Cambridge Elements ≡

Elements in Ancient Egypt in Context
Gianluca Miniaci
University of Pisa
Juan Carlos Moreno García
CNRS, Paris
Anna Stevens
University of Cambridge and Monash University

POWER AND REGIONS IN ANCIENT STATES

An Egyptian and Mesoamerican Perspective

Gary M. Feinman
Field Museum of Natural History, Chicago
Juan Carlos Moreno García
CNRS, Paris

CAMBRIDGE
UNIVERSITY PRESS

CAMBRIDGE
UNIVERSITY PRESS

University Printing House, Cambridge CB2 8BS, United Kingdom

One Liberty Plaza, 20th Floor, New York, NY 10006, USA

477 Williamstown Road, Port Melbourne, VIC 3207, Australia

314–321, 3rd Floor, Plot 3, Splendor Forum, Jasola District Centre, New Delhi – 110025, India

103 Penang Road, #05–06/07, Visioncrest Commercial, Singapore 238467

Cambridge University Press is part of the University of Cambridge.

It furthers the University's mission by disseminating knowledge in the pursuit of education, learning, and research at the highest international levels of excellence.

www.cambridge.org
Information on this title: www.cambridge.org/9781108816229
DOI: 10.1017/9781108907361

© Gary M. Feinman and Juan Carlos Moreno García 2022

First published 2022

A catalogue record for this publication is available from the British Library.

ISBN 978-1-108-81622-9 Paperback
ISSN 2516-4813 (online)
ISSN 2516-4805 (print)

Power and Regions in Ancient States

An Egyptian and Mesoamerican Perspective

Elements in Ancient Egypt in Context

DOI: 10.1017/9781108907361
First published online: February 2022

Gary M. Feinman
Field Museum of Natural History, Chicago

Juan Carlos Moreno García
CNRS, Paris

Author for correspondence: Gary M. Feinman, gfeinman@fieldmuseum.org

Abstract: The aim of this Element is to provide a comprehensive comparison of the basic organization of power in Mesoamerica and Egypt. How power emerged and was exercised, how it reproduced itself, how social units (from households to cities) became integrated into political formation, and how these articulations of power expanded and collapsed over time. The resilience of particular areas (Oaxaca, Middle Egypt), to the point that they preserved a highly distinctive cultural personality when they were or were not included within states, may provide a useful guideline about the basics of integration, negotiation and autonomy in the organization of political formations.

Keywords: ancient Egypt, ancient Mesoamerica, ancient economy, ancient states, geography of power

ISBNs: 9781108816229 (PB), 9781108907361 (OC)
ISSNs: 2516-4813 (online), 2516-4805 (print)

Contents

1 Comparing Ancient Societies: Prehispanic Mesoamerica and the Nilotic World

When we think about historical comparisons between ancient societies across millennia, Mesoamerica and Egypt are rarely brought together. The geographical and temporal distance that separates them is perhaps the most obvious reason why this is seldom done, not to mention that they belonged to two completely different cultural and socioeconomic spheres that had no contact before the mid-second millennium AD. Yet, both terms, "Mesoamerica" and "Egypt," conceal a less obvious but nevertheless crucial feature in their respective configurations of power and economic connectivity that may justify comparing them. Mesoamerica and Egypt designate broad cultural regions, each of them not necessarily unified into a single political entity, even less so limited to a single cultural tradition. In fact, both of these large macroregions encompassed a diversity of regions and numerous cultural identities, to the point that the politico-economic networks and interactions that characterized these broader domains were a key dynamic in change over the long term. At times, in both the Nile Valley and Mesoamerica, political realms were large, encompassing wide swaths of the macroregion, while at other times, local domains were more autonomous.

Our comparative investigation is undertaken at various analytical scales, from the political and economic interests of local actors, to larger institutions and networks that helped define norms and values across these worlds. Such values served to legitimize proper leadership, the right exercise of power, the implementation of justice, and acceptable forms of appropriation and distribution of wealth. In neither region were they fixed or consistent across time or space. Such values were continuously reinterpreted, adapted and used selectively through a dense web of cultural and economic exchanges, negotiations and political interventions that helped shape idiosyncratic identities and build authority. In this vein, the scope of the economic and political interests and interactions of regional actors and institutions led historically to the emergence of diverse political solutions across Mesoamerica and in Egypt, ranging from city-states to regional kingdoms, territorial states and "empires." The discussions in this Element examine long-term changes in local regions and polities as well as the connectivities between them.

Pharaonic Egypt is often interpreted as the earliest territorial state in history, but political division, regional diversity and the emergence of local powers that claimed kingship and fought among themselves for supremacy were also constitutive of its long history. Even in periods of political unity under a single ruler (or pharaoh), some regions and their leaders preserved significant degrees of autonomy and succeeded in limiting the fiscal and political room for central authorities to maneuver (Moreno García 2017, 2018). A comparable but rather more complex pattern emerged in Mesoamerica (Blanton *et al.* 1993:1–13), a vast area encompassing numerous cultural regions (e.g., Maya, Zapotec, Central Highlands, Gulf Coast), each one organized into polities ranging from city-states to local kingdoms (Figure 1). Only during Aztec times, late in the prehispanic era, was a significant sector of Mesoamerica integrated politically.

Given this variability in governance, regions such as Middle Egypt, in the Nile Valley (the area between Memphis and Abydos) (Figure 2), and diverse areas in Mesoamerica may provide fertile ground for comparing how regional leadership emerged and organized itself, what limits were imposed on supraregional rulership, what role trade and control over exchange networks played in the crystallization of such nodes of authority, and what political and economic interests guided the relations of these local powers with their peers as well as with supraregional authorities. Such authorities and the configurations of power that they inspired left their mark on the territories under their control. It may be possible then to discern distinctive patterns of settlement, monumental landscapes, the facilities through which wealth circulated, was accumulated and transformed, and finally, the transformations of the landscape imposed by the fiscal and productive requirements of such authorities. Such marks also expressed the ideological values and actions of rulers (and their critical acceptance or adaptation by common people), the distribution of symbolic goods and power between rulers, whether regional or supraregional (from hierarchical to inter-peer channels), and the forms that this distribution imposed on the dispersal of wealth at local and wider scales. Placed at the crossroads of crucial trade networks in Mesoamerica and the Nile Valley, regions such as the Valley of Oaxaca, the Basin of Mexico, the Usumacinta River corridor (all in Mesoamerica) and Middle Egypt offer a lens that can reveal the challenges, opportunities and limits faced by the historical configurations of power in early polities. This is why we think that pharaonic Middle Egypt and pre-Columbian Mesoamerica represent fruitful arenas for discerning particularities and common features of the organization of power in these premodern societies, particularly when we consider that, in the case of Middle Egypt, this region emerged in some periods as a surprisingly active political player, as its elites provided crucial support to the monarchy against potential rivals based in other areas of Egypt. Actually, it was a recurrent fact in Egyptian history that, in periods of political division, the country was divided into two kingdoms: one usually based in Thebes (Upper Egypt); and the other in Lower Egypt and the immediately adjacent areas. While it is impossible to address these questions in detail within this small volume, such comparison may be productive by

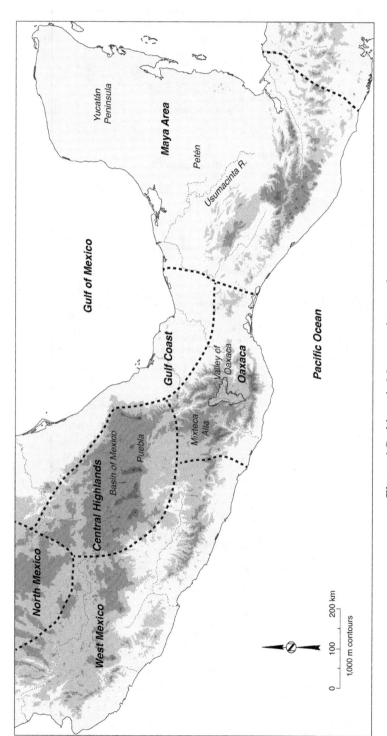

Figure 1 Prehispanic Mesoamerican regions

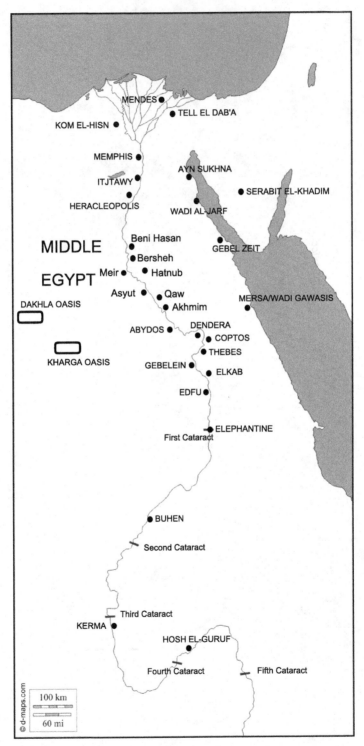

Figure 2 Map of Egypt

focusing our study on broad comparative dimensions of political economy and the rise and organization of authority from technological and economic bases. Our analytical lens is not pointed toward specifically cultural matters.

The study of ancient states is gaining momentum and inspiring more sophisticated analysis. Technological innovations are enhancing the examination and our knowledge of exchange, dating and human landscape usage, as well as population movements. Furthermore, the study of historical states is finally moving beyond the false historical dichotomy that was drawn between the Occidental "West" and the global "rest." Archaeologists and historians are now questioning and abandoning the conceptual frames that have for too long drawn strong demarcations between European history and that of the rest of the globe. Rational social actors did not solely inhabit the West but were universal. That means that researchers cannot merely presume how and why humans cooperate and aggregate at large scales; the basis for these political and economic affiliations must be explained, and the differences over time and space accounted for. Although this is not a simple endeavor, archaeologists and ancient historians have an advantage, relevant to the present. In studying the past, we cannot only flesh out socioeconomic mechanisms and relationships between different institutions but we can examine the outcomes from different organizational parameters, something less viable for present cases.

Far from considering ancient tributary (or, simply, non-Western) states as autocracies subject to the arbitrary power and tax demands of their rulers, recent research is increasingly focused on the changing infrastructural organization and the balance of power between different actors that made the very existence of such political entities possible and viable. Not by chance, ancient China and ancient Rome have received considerable attention in comparative historical studies. On the one hand, Rome represents a divergent path that led ultimately to the rise of modern capitalism and the modern state in the "West." On the other hand, China's millennial state organization is producing a distinctive path toward industrialization and capitalism. Other studies are increasingly aware of the limits of earlier explanations about the "origins" of the state. One can think, for instance, of the model elaborated and popularized by Gordon Childe (1950), in which urbanization, craft specialization, division of labor, writing and social hierarchy, among other elements, went hand in hand. Alternative views, based on the exponential accumulation of archaeological data, on more refined methods in the analysis of textual data, and on the increasing integration of theories and methods from social sciences, make it possible to compare the historical trajectories of ancient states and, in doing so, to discern structural elements underlying the emergence, dynamics and organization of power in early polities (Scheidel 2015; Ando and Richardson 2017; Brooke, Strauss and Anderson 2018; Yoffee 2019; Graeber and Wengrow 2021).

No longer can we presume that historical states simply formed when homogenous, neighboring peoples coalesced out of interest for the good of the group as a whole. Likewise, we can no longer suppose that the boundaries of states and other early polities were fixed, closed and immutable over time. Ancient worlds were composed of networks, social, political and economic, and sometimes overlapping. Central questions that we must ask are: How was political power funded? How did differences in the fiscal foundations of different states affect the nature of leadership? What factors enhanced or limited the scope of rulership and power?

Contrary to rather common stereotypes about pharaonic Egypt as a homogeneous society that survived for three millennia almost unaltered, under (apparently) a single political form (a monarchy headed by a king), increasing evidence has been marshalled to illustrate that under the cover of tradition and royal continuity, the very foundations of kingship and of the state underwent intense changes over three millennia (Baines and Yoffee 1998; Moreno García 2018, 2019a). Even the very existence of Egypt as a single kingdom for most of its history was neither an inevitable nor "the natural" condition that power took in the northern section of the Nile Valley, extending from Aswan to the Mediterranean. Other possibilities were also available, and it is quite possible that the political landscape of Lower Egypt (the Delta region), for instance, shared more characteristics with the southern Levant than with Upper Egypt. Extensive trade contacts with foreign territories, political fragmentation, extensive herding and fluctuating urbanism punctuated by periods of abandonment of settlements recall similar conditions that prevailed in neighboring areas in Southwest Asia, like Syria and Canaan. As a hub between, precisely, Upper Egypt and the Delta, Middle Egypt was essential in any project to (re)build a single authority over the country. So, far from the impression of massive autocratic power and centralization of resources suggested by the pyramids of Giza or the huge temples of Thebes, it was the historical combinations of regional powers that finally resulted (or not) in the emergence of a single state. Finally, the accumulation of fresh archaeological data reveal that Nubia, another political actor in the Nilotic world, was a major power in northeast Africa, capable of intervening in Egyptian affairs and influencing the Egyptian political map in some periods. Far from being a backward region, only prone to Egyptian expansionism in search for precious goods, Nubian polities represented a formidable rival for pharaonic interest, capable of interfering in the internal affairs of Egypt (for instance in Middle Egypt), providing support to some Egyptian factions and polities against others, controlling its own exchange networks toward the Mediterranean and the Horn of Africa, and conquering Egypt if necessary (Smith 2013).

Although the Nilotic world was less politically unified and centralized than often presumed, it still was far more so than ancient Mesoamerica. Even the metropolis of Teotihuacan at its height during the first millennium AD was politically dominant over a relatively small sector of Mesoamerica, not that much beyond the Basin of Mexico (Hirth *et al.* 2020). Monte Albán (Blanton 1978), the dominant early center in the Valley of Oaxaca, also controlled a small territory, which appears to have shrunk during its lengthy political hegemony. The Classic Maya cities, which featured principles of divine, kingly leadership that parallel Egypt in certain ways, had mostly small political realms that tended to be relatively short-lived, no more than a few centuries. Only the later Aztec politically dominated a larger segment of Mesoamerica, but much of that world was still beyond its dominance when the Spanish arrived. Although there are notable exceptions, political leadership in Mesoamerica tended to have less concentrated power and individual aggrandizement than that found in Egypt. We endeavor to understand these differences in terms of resources and how economies were institutionally organized/controlled.

The remainder of this Element is divided into seven additional sections. We begin by defining the two macroregions and their subdivisions, and then proceed to the conceptual frames and multiscalar perspectives that we bring to this comparative work. In the remaining sections, we discuss elements of time/space variation across these two historical realms, drawing points of contrast and parallel between them.

2 Regional Background

The preindustrial Mesoamerican and Egyptian worlds were roughly comparable in areal size, both just over 1,000,000 square kilometers (including the deserts surrounding the Nile Valley; however, the habitable space in Egypt and the oases was roughly about 25,000 square kilometers). But geographically, they were highly diverse. The Nilotic world was centered on the longest river in the world, which flows from south to north. In contrast, Mesoamerica is highly diverse both topographically and vegetationally, including high mountain ranges, highland valleys, and both wet and dry lowland zones (Blanton *et al.* 1993:4–7).

2.1 Landscape and Natural Environment in Middle Egypt

At Egypt's north was the Nile Delta or Lower Egypt (Figure 2). South of the Delta is Middle Egypt (roughly, from Lake Fayum to the city of Akhmim), which divides the low-lying waterlogged north from the narrower stretches of the Nile Valley, known as Upper Egypt. For much of its early history, Middle Egypt had a core political and economic role in the Nilotic world (Moreno García 2017). Even from a geographical and physical point of view, Middle Egypt exhibits some distinctive features that set it apart from the rest of the Nile Valley and that may help explain its influence in the political history of pharaonic Egypt (Moreno García 2021). Middle Egypt is crossed both by the Nile and the Bahr Yussef, the canal that connects the river with the Fayum and runs parallel to the Nile for about 220 kilometers from Dairut to Fayum. Middle Egypt was a region rich in pastureland and marshes. It was also the point of arrival of several desert routes that connected the Nile Valley to northern Nubia as well as to the string of oases of the Western (or Libyan) Desert, situated around 200–400 kilometers west of the Nile. This array of water sources provided an alternative way of communication and exchange to the Nile. Not by chance, peoples living in the Western Desert and in Nubia arrived and frequented Middle Egypt. Occasionally, they were represented in the tombs of the elites that ruled this area and, judging from the written record, they also played an important political role, at least during certain periods of the pharaonic past. Another particular feature of this region is that, contrary to the relatively broad strip of the valley west of the river (the area between the Bahr Yussef and the Nile), the Eastern Desert drops abruptly down to the Nile for most of Middle Egypt. Hence, cultivable land is reduced to a minimum along the east bank between the area immediately north of Asyut/Deir el-Gebrawy and the Fayum, a problem exacerbated by the historical move of the Nile to the east in this region. This may explain the strategic importance of Asyut (its name literally means "sentinel") as the key entrance point or "doorway" into Middle Egypt from the south.

Recent research also reveals that various additional branches of the Nile and hydrological arteries existed in Middle Egypt between the Nile and the Bahr Yussef. Furthermore, due to the profile of the floodplain, only a relatively small part of the flood water could drain back into the Nile after the flood season because it remained trapped between the levees of the Nile and the Bahr Yussef. Therefore, an irregular system of waterways existed in the area between Bersheh and the entrance to the Fayum, while large accumulations of water remained there long after the end of the flood season. So, the existence of a vast wet zone between the Nile and the Bahr Yussef south of the Fayum made most of this area unsuitable for the cultivation of cereals as much as for habitation, to the point that even in the eighteenth century AD it was still thinly populated (Willems *et al.* 2017). Things were not much different south of Bersheh (Gillam 2010). Distinctive crop marks in fields to the south and to the north of El-Qusiya suggest a hydrological origin. They also occurred in high concentrations in a band along the western edge of the valley in the vicinity of Meir. Elongated plots of land sometimes associated with these features can be identified as filled-in canals. Both of these features have also been found elsewhere and have been interpreted as a network of braided channels, representing the waterways and swamps that tended to pool in the low-lying edges of the convex alluvial floodplain (Trampier 2005/2006). Another feature is the existence of abandoned levees between two and four kilometers from the present location of the Nile bed near El-Qusiya. So, in premodern times, the western bank of the Nile in many areas of Middle Egypt appears to have been a complex landscape of waterways, canals and abandoned levees with a strong presence of marshes. Finally, silt and sediments carried by the annual flood of the Nile created islands, usually close to the western bank of the Nile, that became gradually covered by vegetation. Probably not by chance, officials in charge of the administration and cultivation of "new islands" and "new localities" are particularly well documented in Middle Egypt, as this region happened to be a sort of "colonization front," an ideal area to expand agriculture, but susceptible to return to a flooded condition if drainage and terracing works were not regularly kept. As time passed on, siltation filled the channels that separated these islands from the mainland and contributed to expand the floodplain and to displace the Nile further to the East (Moreno García 2013a).

Finally, the "moving landscape" resulting from these particular ecological and environmental conditions may explain why Middle Egypt presents a rather differentiated organization in terms of settlement density and structure, as well as of productive activities, with its core situated between Asyut in the south and Bersheh in the north (Bunbury 2019). North of Bersheh, the density of human occupation seems to fall dramatically, at least until the Ramesside period (1292–1077 BC). In fact, human occupation in this relatively vast area was quite unequal, and the presence of the crown and its local agents was based, in many periods of Egyptian history, on a patchy network of small urban sites and royal administrative/economic centers, scattered over a large area and separated by bushy and marshy areas as well as pastures (Antoine 2017; Moreno García 2020). This means that one of the most persistent myths about ancient Egypt, that the central power organized irrigation at a large scale and promoted hydraulic works in order to monitor the seasonal flood of the Nile and divert water from the river to the fields, should be disregarded. Traces of any centralized control of the flood or irrigation system are absent for the period considered. In fact, agriculture and irrigation were managed at a very local level and the interventions of the state, if any, were reduced to a minimum. Even irrigation canals and dikes are quite rare in the administrative and archaeological record (Moreno García 2019a:53). So, when Nekhebu, an official who lived around 2300 BC, claimed in the inscriptions of his tomb that "his majesty sent me to lay out a canal in the (area of) Akhbit of Horus and to excavate it. I excavated it in a period of three months, so that when I came back to the Residence it was already full of water" and "his majesty sent me to Kis to excavate his canal (?) for (goddess) Hathor-in-Kis. I acted and excavated it so that his majesty favored me for it" (Strudwick 2005:265–266), the purpose of such hydraulic works remains ambiguous: irrigation, navigation, drainage or supply of fresh water?

As a consequence, land irrigation mostly depended on the flood, with minimal arrangement of the natural basins in the floodplain, while natural wells and ponds contributed to the cultivation of small gardens and plots of land in the immediate surroundings of settlements. The resulting agricultural landscape was thus not a continuous succession of cultivated fields in a homogeneously laid out floodplain crossed by artificial dikes, channels, sluices and roads. It was a more "natural" environment instead, a patchwork of fields and villages created where the natural conditions of the river permitted (circulation of the flood, presence of levees, good draining conditions, etc.). The determinant factor in the agricultural cycle was the annual inundation of the Nile. Depending on the height of the flood, the resulting landscape, the extent of the irrigated areas and the volume of the harvest experienced important variations from one year to the next. Given the crucial importance of the flood, it provided the basis for the Egyptian calendar with its three seasons: *akhet*, "the flooding" (mid-July to mid-November), when the inundation covered the fertile riverbanks (the actual flood took place from mid-July to October) and canals could be opened to water higher land; *peret*, "the coming forth" (mid-November to mid-March), when plowing, sowing and germination took place; and *shemu*, "harvest" (mid-March to mid-July), when the harvest was gathered (Moreno García 2020).

2.2 The Emergence of Social Complexity in Middle Egypt

Overall, Middle Egypt was a microcosm that encompassed some of the most distinctive characteristics of the Nile Valley: an abundance of potential agricultural land but also of pasture and marsh areas susceptible (at least in part) to cultivation; a crossroads of river and land routes; easy connections with the neighboring desert areas; and, finally, an eventful history made of changes in the patterns of occupation of the territory, in the emergence of new types of settlement, in the foundation of agricultural estates and of "colonies" of foreigners, and in the oscillation between the expansion of agricultural areas (often under the initiative of the crown) and their subsequent contraction followed by a return to more mobile lifestyles (pastoralism, fishing, fowl hunting, etc.). However, little is known about the development of agriculture, sedentary life and urbanism in this region before 2500 BC, when archaeological and epigraphic sources became relatively abundant. It was commonly assumed that in an otherwise rather sparse Neolithic archaeological record, the concentration of early Neolithic (Badarian) cemeteries in Middle Egypt was exceptional and pointed to the vitality of village life in this region in the fifth millennium BC. Recent archaeological research reveals that it was not the case. In fact, these cemeteries correspond to a cultural landscape in which ancestral burial grounds reveal two phenomena, the emergence of new forms of territoriality and the changing location of seasonal herding and fishing camps along the margins of the floodplain, which reflects high levels of residential mobility among herder-fisher-forager populations (Horn 2017). Only later, in the early fourth millennium BC, did traces of cereal farming and sedentary life – such as durable architecture, heavy plant processing equipment and high proportions of cereal grains in botanical samples – make their first appearance in the Egyptian Nile Valley, but they are poorly attested in Middle Egypt. By contrast, the Eastern Delta and southernmost Egypt (Abydos, Naqada, Hierakonpolis, Elkab) were then the most dynamic areas in Egypt (Stevenson 2016). It was only in the first centuries of the third millennium BC when cemeteries (Asyut, Bersheh, Beni Hasan) and occasional monumental architecture (rock-tombs, a small step pyramid) reveal the presence of a local elite in Middle Egypt, well connected with the central power based then at Memphis. Epigraphic evidence confirms this picture. Local potentates referred to as governors of the province of the Oryx (the area of Beni Hasan) delivered offerings to the mortuary monuments of kings living around 2700 BC (Vanthuyne 2018; Moreno García 2019a). Judging from slightly later archaeological evidence, it seems that the exploitation of the calcite quarries in Middle Egypt and the need to create the logistics indispensable to feed and equip the teams of workers sent there were major incentives in the emergence of such local elites (an example: Willems 2009).

Under these conditions, one of the main political and economic assets of Middle Egypt was control over trade routes and, consequently, close contacts and alliances with peoples living along them, such as Nubians, Libyans and others with links to Asia. From a political point of view, this means that local leaders from Middle Egypt might develop their own interests and strategies, seeking either to influence the central authority of the state or to follow an autonomous policy, even to establish their own agreements with foreign actors in order to assert such interests and strategies. This, in turn, means that the integration of this region in the political structure of the kingdom was far from granted and that, consequently, pharaohs or regional kings (when the central monarchy collapsed) had to cope with the authorities of Middle Egypt using diverse means, ranging from negotiation to the crude use of force (Moreno García 2017). Another consequence is that the ways in which these authorities were finally integrated into the kingdom had the potential to challenge the tax system of the monarchy. This is especially evident when the interests of kings and local nobles clashed, when local nobles diverted for themselves revenue that, under "normal" conditions, should have filled the state coffers, or when they continued to control crucial economic circuits even after the reunification of the country – and to derive income from them. In the long term, local nobles could thus limit the implementation of royal fiscal policies and royal authority locally. In these cases, they may consolidate their position as autonomous poles of accumulation of wealth and power that restricted the scope of royal authority in the areas under their control. The occasional presence of Nubian, Asiatic and Libyan warriors in the retinues of some Middle Egypt nobles, the support that these nobles gave to pharaohs seeking to assert their power over Egypt, or, inversely, the assistance provided by Nubians and Asiatics to rebels from Middle Egypt reveal the complexities of the organization of power in Egypt. Far from being simply the pure expression of royal will, the construction of a central power and a unique royal authority was a painstaking process based on negotiation, on a delicate balance of power between diverse actors and on the harmonization of interests not necessarily convergent (Moreno García 2017, 2018).

In the end, the configurations of power, the modalities of production and accumulation of wealth in Middle Egypt and the integration of this section of the Nile Valley into supraregional political entities (mainly, but not only, the pharaonic monarchy) appear as part of a dynamic process. Local actors may or may not choose to be part of a state, and, when they decided to do so, it was not rare that they imposed their own conditions, which is what happened when the elites buried at Beni Hasan and Bersheh joined the Theban kingdom around 2050 BC, but on the condition of retaining much control over Egyptian foreign trade (Moreno García 2017). But, at the same time, kings managed crucial tools that helped influence and shape those local actors in order to "align" their interests with those of the monarchy. Interventions in provincial temples (providers of both income and legitimacy to local elites) was one of them, together with the promotion of agricultural expansion; the integration of local elites into the administration of the state (thus broadening the scope of their expectations and their sources of income); a policy of intermarrying with provincial families (Kanawati 2017); providing support to local subelites as a way to weaken the authority of provincial lords; and, finally, by promoting some members of powerful local kin groups to the detriment of others in order to break the solidarity of the group and to promote individualist strategies akin to the interest of the monarchy. Middle Egypt thus provides a privileged lens to analyze the organization of power in ancient Egypt at the crossroads of trade, economy, politics and interaction with diverse populations (nomads, foreign peoples, etc.). The Nile was at the core, and the resources that were carried along this watercourse underpinned the concentrations of wealth and political clout (Moreno García 2018).

2.3 Mesoamerica: Landscapes and Populations

Although access to water was critical in prehispanic Mesoamerica, the area was not focused on a single landscape feature, like the Nile. Rather, Mesoamerica was a mosaic of mountains, valleys, coastal plains, rainforests and volcanos. To the north, it was roughly defined by the deserts of northern Mexico and the drainage of the Pánuco–Lerma Rivers, so that only the southern two-thirds of the country is considered part of Mesoamerica. The southern limits of this macroregion were less finite and more variable over time, with the Ulúa River and Lake Yojoa marking a temporally fleeting edge. Nevertheless, it is critical to realize that despite the absence of beasts of burden in prehispanic Mesoamerica, communication and economic flows were a regular feature between Mesoamerica and the neighboring worlds, both to the north and south. Likewise, although we speak of different language and ethnic populations in prehispanic Mesoamerica, such as Maya, Zapotec, Mixtec, and others, neither the topographic features nor cultural distinctions between polities and peoples served as impenetrable, uncrossable boundaries (Blanton *et al.* 1993:4–10).

Unlike the Nilotic world, the landscape of Mesoamerica was topographically diverse and fragmented, split by a series of high mountain ranges, the Central Mexican Highlands, the Southern Highlands, and the Guatemalan Highlands. Between these clusters of mountains were large highland valleys, including the Basin of Mexico and the Valley of Oaxaca. The Basin surrounded a large lake, now mostly drained, that is the setting today for the large metropolis of Mexico City. The Valley of Oaxaca, roughly half the size of the Basin of Mexico, is trisected by the Atoyac River and its tributary the Salado River. Because of their flat land and access to water, these semiarid, large highland valleys were draws for prehispanic settlement, as were smaller highland valleys in both the Central and Southern Highlands.

At lower elevations than the high mountain zones and the semiarid valleys were Mesoamerican lowland areas, which were situated along the coasts of the Gulf of Mexico and Pacific Ocean, as well as the relatively flat plain that runs from the Yucatán Peninsula to the wetter, more heavily vegetated Petén and the

Isthmus of Tehuantepec, a flat narrow strip that connected the Gulf and the Pacific. Mesoamerica's longest river, the Usumacinta, runs northwest across the lowlands from the Guatemala Highlands to the Gulf. Like the Nile, the Usumacinta River had a significant role in the region's history. But the river's importance was most impactful during the era when the prehispanic Maya centers of the Classic period (AD 250–900) predominated.

Mesoamerica is one of the most biodiverse regions of the world, with snowcapped volcanic peaks, arid plains, semiarid valleys and lush, forested lowlands. Yet, one plant, corn (*Zea mays*), an adaptable domesticate, is and was the key agrarian resource that linked the peoples of Mesoamerica (Kirchhoff 1943). Where corn could be reliably grown, prehispanic Mesoamerican peoples settled at least for a time. The prehispanic populations of this world supplemented corn with many other domesticated and wild plants. The former included beans, squash, tomatoes, avocados and cacao, but in most Mesoamerican regions from early sedentary settlements to the sixteenth-century arrival of the Spanish, maize provided a sizable caloric contribution. In drier, more drought-prone parts of Mesoamerica, xerophytic plants such as maguey (agave), yucca, nopal and a variety of other succulents were also essential dietary elements.

Animal foods, particularly domestic animals, were less prominent in prehispanic Mesoamerica than they were in Egypt or other centers of early urban societies around the globe. The only animals that ultimately were domesticated in prehispanic Mesoamerica were the dog, the turkey, honeybees and, perhaps, cottontail rabbits. Many Mesoamerican peoples also supplemented their fields by hunting wild animals, such as deer, jackrabbits and peccary. The absence of domesticated herd animals not only had implications for diet, transport and farming methods, but it also meant that the interactive dynamic between farmers and herders so key to the history of societies in Eurasia and Africa was not central to the prehispanic Mesoamerican past. Nevertheless, at specific times and places, such as at the time of the Aztec empire (ca. AD 1325–1521), certain prehispanic Mesoamerica peoples focused heavily on xerophytic plants and the products that were made with them, including fiber, pigment and alcohol, thereby establishing symbiotic links with nearby and adjacent communities that relied more heavily on farming corn.

The peoples of prehispanic Mesoamerica also differed from many other early urban societies in their reliance on stone tool technologies. Metallurgy was not evidenced in the macroregion until roughly AD 700. But, even after that date, most uses of metal were ornamental or as media of exchange, such as the copper axes in Aztec times, and the material was rarely fashioned into production-related tools. Although prehispanic Mesoamerican farmers devised a plethora of ingenious ways to bring water to their fields, including pot irrigation, raised fields, irrigation systems, check dams and floodwater farming, most of these systems were relatively small in scale and could be managed at a local level. An exception was at the time of the Aztec empire, when larger-scale water control systems were employed to tap and control the lake system in the Basin of Mexico.

As with farming systems, most craft production in prehispanic Mesoamerica was household-based (Feinman and Nicholas 2012). There is relatively little indication that larger-scale nondomestic workshop or factory production was evidenced before the arrival of the Spanish. In larger Mesoamerican urban contexts, such as at Teotihuacan (Millon 1973), a Classic-period metropolis in Central Mexico, craft producers may have had their labor taxed in order to produce for temples or other institutions, but this seems to have been just a part-time commitment. Nevertheless, although the scale of production in Mesoamerica tended to be small, situated domestically, produced in part for exchange and often sold in markets, these economic relations have a deep history in this global region. Community and household economic interdependence extend back to the beginnings of sedentary life in Mesoamerica, and markets, despite the difficulty of documenting them archaeologically, also seem to have a deep history in the region, certainly at least back to the Classic period (Kowalewski 2019). When the Spanish arrived at the Aztec capital (Tenochtitlán), they gushed and expounded extensively over the size and diversity of the central market at Tlatelolco, Tenochtitlán's sister city, noting that it was grander than any market they knew in the Mediterranean world. The enormous Tlatelolco market, which was the hub of an extensive regional market system, likely had roots in earlier prehispanic economic systems, for which archaeologists are increasingly finding evidence of marketplace exchange (Hirth 2016).

Our comparison here of two areas characterized by early urbanism draws on approximately 3,000–3,500 years of history (see Table 1 and Table 2) for both the prehispanic Mesoamerican and Nilotic worlds. Nevertheless, the specific years covered are not equivalent. In each microregion, we begin with the advent of early sedentary villages, which happened earlier in Egypt, and carry the discussion forward to a major episode of change that altered macroregional history. For Egypt, our focus is between 4600 BC and roughly 1250 BC, when Egypt's capital was moved from Middle Egypt to the Delta. In Mesoamerica, we begin our historical examination around 2000 BC and end the coverage with Spanish conquest, which occurred early in the sixteenth century, with catastrophic demographic ramifications for people across this world. The next section explores these issues.

Table 1 Chronology and major events in Egypt

Period	Dates	Political situation
Early Unified Monarchy	3100–2613 BC	Narmer, from Abydos, became the first pharaoh of a unified Egypt (capital: Memphis, Lower Egypt).
Old Kingdom	2613–2345 BC	Centralization of power under the hegemony of the king's family (capital: Memphis). Later on, the state expanded its basis of power gradually through the incorporation of "new men" and a more active presence in the provinces.
Late Old Kingdom	2345–2160 BC	Increasing importance of the provinces as well as of the role of Egypt as a provider of gold, ivory, exotic hides (from Nubia) and textiles to the Near East (Byblos, Ebla).
First Intermediate Period	2160–2055 BC	Two kingdoms: Heracleopolis (Lower and Middle Egypt) and Thebes (Upper Egypt). International trade expanded.
Reunification by Theban pharaoh Mentuhotep II	2055–2004 BC (actual date still debated)	Conquest of Heracleopolis and reunification of the country (capital: Thebes, Upper Egypt).
Early Middle Kingdom	2004–1800 BC	Unified monarchy (capital: Itjtawy; just south of Memphis). Nubia unified for the first time as the kingdom of Kush (capital: Kerma). Extensive trade with Nubia, the Aegean and the Levant.
Late Middle Kingdom	1800–1750 BC	Quick succession of many kings on the throne. Beginning of the fragmentation of the country.
Second Intermediate Period	1750–1550 BC	Egypt divided into two monarchies: the Hyksos in the north (capital: Avaris, in northeastern Lower Egypt) and Thebes in the south. Avaris became one of the main trade hubs of the Eastern Mediterranean.

Table 2 Chronology and major events in Mesoamerica

Period	Dates	Political situation
Archaic	9000–2000 BC	Mobile populations organized in fluid, low-density bands and reliant mainly on wild resources, supplemented by cultigens.
Early Formative	2000–900 BC	Advent of sedentary settlements in many, but not all, regions, associated with the construction of diverse forms of public architecture and hierarchical supra-household social relations. The most monumental construction is on the Gulf Coast.
Middle Formative	900–300 BC	Rise of early cities, such as Monte Albán in the Valley of Oaxaca. Large demographic aggregations and increasingly hierarchical forms of sociopolitical complexity emerged across much of Mesoamerica.
Late/Terminal Formative	300 BC–AD 300	Teotihuacan established as the largest city of its time. Rise of Maya lords at central settlements across the lowland Maya region.
Early Classic	AD 300–600	Increasing urbanism and population density across Mesoamerica. Teotihuacan, Maya centers, such as Tikal, and Monte Albán dominated their respective regions. Forms of governance, urban layouts and investments in monumental architecture were highly variable.
Late Classic	AD 600–900	Disaggregation and political breakdown at Teotihuacan ramified across Mesoamerica, prompting growth of settlements in some regions and decline in others. By the end of this period, Monte Albán and many of the Classic Maya cities suffered episodes of marked decline.
Early Postclassic	AD 900–1200	An episode of macroscale reorganization. New centers arose (Tula) or grew markedly in significance (Chichén Itzá) in many regions, but they generally were smaller than the largest metropolises of the Classic period. Across much of the Central and Southern Highlands, networks of small statelets competed for predominance.
Late Postclassic	AD 1200–1500	Establishment and rapid growth of Tenochtitlán at the core of the Aztec empire. The empire fostered new connectivities across much of the Mesoamerican world, even beyond its political extents.

3 The Economic Basis: Agriculture, Sedentary Life and Productive Complexity

3.1 Royal Centers and Elusive Cities in Middle Egypt

One of the most striking differences between ancient Middle Egypt and pre-hispanic Mesoamerica concerns sedentary life and the different paths that were taken to urbanism in the two regions. For most of the pharaonic period, Middle Egypt was characterized by a marshy environment, favorable for cattle raising and, potentially, for agricultural expansion. Human occupation in this relatively vast area was spatially unequal, so the authority of the crown and of its local collaborators was based, in many periods of Egyptian history, on a patchy network of temples, small urban sites and royal administrative/economic centers, scattered over the Nile Valley and separated by shrubby and water-logged areas. Until at least 2000 BC, mobile lifestyles apparently prevailed in this region, while urbanism, as it also happened in most of Egypt, was limited (Moreno García 2017). Only the locality of Zawiyet el-Mayetin provides some limited hints about what urban life would have been like in this region in the third millennium BC, and the pattern shows many commonalities with other areas of Egypt. On the one hand, early urbanism seems closely associated with the presence of the crown in this area. A small step pyramid close to Zawiyet el-Mayetin and some inscribed tombs and pottery remains found nearby suggest that this site was a center of elite power around 2600 BC. Later on, roughly between 2450 and 2200 BC, the elite that dominated this site made themselves more visible in the archaeological record thanks to its monuments and its decorated tombs, often inscribed with the rank and function titles held by its most prominent members and decorated according to the artistic codes of the palatial culture of this period. On the other hand, the period between 2200 and 2000 BC witnessed some expansion of the settled area at Zawiyet el-Mayetin, but it is impossible to evaluate the magnitude of this phenomenon (Moeller 2005; Bussmann 2019).

The example of Zawiyet el-Mayetin seems representative of similar developments that took place at other sites of Middle Egypt in the same period but are much less well documented. In the absence of significant archaeological evidence about cities and settlements, not to speak of administrative or economic documents, elite cemeteries with costly decorated inscribed tombs are the best evidence for the existence of a stratified society whose ruling elite was closely linked to the crown. Local inscriptions mention settlements, but their actual size, layout and economic diversity (if any) is simply unknown. It may be probable that these sites were not unsubstantial nevertheless, as they were inhabited at least by officials, administrators, their families and retinues, the craftsmen that decorated their tombs and the workers occupied in the production and transformation of agricultural produce subsequently stored in the administrative and economic centers of the crown. According to evidence dating to about 2300–2200 BC, many dozens of people were part of the retinue of the most important nobles buried at sites such as Meir or Sharuna. So, one can imagine that settlements oscillating between at least five and ten hectares were not an oddity in Middle Egypt, and that their tiny dimensions were similar to those of other "urban" sites in Upper Egypt during the late third millennium BC. A particularity of Middle Egypt is that a substantial number of modest rock circle tombs has been discovered close to Beni Hasan and Bersheh. In the case of the latter, these burials formed clusters at the foot of the hills, and each one of these clusters seems associated with one of the small elite rock tombs situated at the top of the escarpments that date from 2600–2500 BC. The rock circle tombs are interpreted as graveyards for the people living in the villages of this area (De Meyer *et al.* 2011; Vanthuyne 2016). So, it seems that in some places, villagers buried in rock circle tombs were integrated into patronage networks that were dominated by a local elite that was buried in rock tombs similar to those found near the capital, at Memphis, and well connected with the royal court.

It appears then that cities and towns hardly grew organically in Middle Egypt in the early and middle third millennium BC, so their development followed the institutional initiatives of the crown, which included, principally, the foundation of royal agricultural and administrative centers called *hwt* and "great *hwt*," a sort of residential, administrative storage building or complex surrounded by extensive fields and provided with workers and cattle. It seems that, originally, a *hwt* was a prestige residential building with the aspect of a tower. These centers were created by the state, which imposed the production of specific homogeneous forms of pottery of a standard size. The pottery recovered at several sites in Middle Egypt consisted of standard bread molds, storage jars and pottery similar to those found in many other areas of Egypt. The local relevance of these settlements and agricultural centers may be only inferred from the epigraphic evidence related to the officials that controlled the *hwt* and the great *hwt*. Towns and *hwt*/great *hwt* appear thus as true "islands of authority" in this region. And, judging from the periodical shifts of the main necropolis from one place to another, it seems that authority circulated in Middle Egypt depending on the political fortunes and the balance of power between the dominant families residing there and between them and the king (Moreno García 2021). This brings forward another problem for the analysis of the settlement structure in this region. The fact that distinctive necropolis were used by specific categories of officials means that the number of elite cemeteries in a given province does not correspond necessarily to that of the actual towns/ cities in it: high and low officials may well have resided in the same locality while being buried in separate cemeteries. In other cases, shifts of power between powerful families led to the abandonment of certain ancestral burial areas and the emergence of others. In any case, the initiatives taken by these families and the ties that they established with the royal administration, oscillating between autonomy and selective integration, had enduring consequences on the settlement organization, the management of the territory and the productive priorities prevalent in Middle Egypt. The traces of such policies may be inferred from the changes of the administrative titles held by the elites buried in Middle Egypt as well as from occasional archaeological evidence about specialized sites (De Meyer 2011a; Moreno García 2021).

The institutional impetus behind the emergence and/or development of towns, cities and administrative centers of the crown in Middle Egypt seemed to pursue three goals. Firstly, to provide the logistics necessary to equip and provision the teams of workers sent to the quarries in this area to obtain the raw materials used in luxury craftsmanship (stone vessels, high-quality buildings, etc.). Secondly, to expand (and stock) agricultural production through the foundation of estates (referred to as "new localities"). And, thirdly, to create infrastructures (harbor facilities, storage areas) where taxes delivered to the state or to institutions could be easily gathered, stored and transported, including manpower. Hundreds of stone vessels buried in the galleries of the pyramid of King Djeser (around 2700 BC) bear inscriptions that mention the names and administrative titles of the officials who presented these offerings to the tomb of the pharaoh. The information that they provide about the early local administration of Egypt is not only invaluable, but it also shows that the province of Beni Hasan, in Middle Egypt, was the only one in all of Egypt headed by a "governor" (*heqa*) and that agricultural centers of the crown (basically the great *hwt*; also *hwt*) represented the main administrative and fiscal units of the state in the provinces together with the "house(holds)" of prominent people (not necessarily officials of the king) and the "(watching) towers"/"forts" that seemed to monitor routes to the deserts (Moreno García 2021). Archaeology has revealed a work processing area close to Bersheh (around 2550 BC) that specialized in quarrying and treating calcite, whereas the alabaster quarries at Hatnub, in the Eastern Desert, had been exploited since 2580 BC (Willems 2009). In both cases, royal expeditions sent teams of stone workers, prospectors and craftsmen there in order to extract specially coveted types of stone used in the production of stone vessels and statues and in the construction of tombs and other monuments.

The possibilities for agricultural expansion in Middle Egypt may then explain why members of the royal family possessed substantial landed assets in this region (Figure 3). The will of Prince Nykaure (aroud 2540 BC) describes his sharing out of several domains to his wife, children and other members of his kin, located both in the Delta and in Middle Egypt, whereas a distinctive branch of the administration managed the domains (house(holds)) of the royal children there. That is why many "new localities" (in fact, new agricultural domains) were founded there (Moreno García 2021). The annual flood of the Nile deposited silt and sediments that formed islands that were subsequently covered by vegetation. Their size could be rather considerable, and these islands provided excellent fertile land in which kings created agricultural holdings (Moreno García 2013a; Bunbury 2019). The titles of several officials who lived in the third and early second millennium BC as well as administrative papyri from the second half of the second millennium BC reveal that the "new agricultural holdings" were a conspicuous mark of Middle Egypt. They also reveal that the work of clearing, leveling and preparing the ground for cultivation was a strenuous task that, in many cases, fell on criminals and soldiers. The papyri show that clusters of agricultural holdings were provided with quays and threshing areas in which grain was collected, stored and delivered to the vessels dispatched by the crown or by the temples to pick it (Moreno García 2013a).

Figure 3 Agricultural landscape at Beni Hasan. Olaf Tausch, CC BY 3.0 https:// creativecommons.org/licenses/by/3.0, via Wikimedia Commons

Temples represented another crucial institution in the management of the territory and its resources. It seems that in the third millennium BC, provincial temples were quite modest buildings, judging by their size and decoration. They were in the hands of powerful local families, and the intervention of the crown in their affairs was limited but highly selective. Being institutions that provided income, legitimacy and prestige, kings used provincial temples as political and economic tools that enabled the crown to penetrate into the local sphere and its complex social networks, to coopt its dominant families and to shape the elites present there. Two measures served this purpose. On the one hand, royal donations of land provided temples with additional resources that increased the income of the elites that managed them. New agricultural holdings, created in formerly flooded areas or in new islands, were ideal for this purpose. On the other hand, kings built chapels equipped with royal statues in these temples and granted priestly titles to their ritualists, thus recognizing officially (and enhancing the status) of the families that managed the sanctuaries. Temples and the production centers of the crown became thus the main managerial and economic institutions in the provinces, and it was not rare that selected local officials controlled both of them. The inscriptions in the tomb of Nykaankh at Tehna or the royal decree for Iaib at Bersheh are proof of this policy. In the first case, Nykaankh accumulated the functions of overseer of a great *hwt*, overseer of the new localities and "overseer of priests of (goddess) Hathor." Other inscriptions in his tomb are full of details about the management of the temple of Hathor. In fact, Nykaankh, his family and acquaintances controlled all of the (remunerated) priestly positions of the temple, and he even stated that King Menkaure had donated half a hectare of land to provide income for the priesthoods, a measure ratified by King Userkaf (Moreno García 2021). As for Iaib, he inscribed at the entrance of his tomb at Bersheh the decree issued by King Reneferef in which he granted several court and priestly titles to him (De Meyer 2011b).

Finally, two major features characterize the economy and settlement organization of Middle Egypt: trade and mobile populations. The area between Asyut and Bersheh/Beni Hasan was the arriving point of desert routes that linked the Nile Valley to the oases of the Western Desert. At the same time, these tracks were used by pastoral populations that frequented the Nile Valley with their herds in search of pasture land and water. That is why provincial authorities promoted the expansion of cattle raising in Middle Egypt, a process particularly well documented from the very end of the third millennium BC. It was then that extensive cattle raising became frequently attested in the sources as well as a new kind of settlement in this region, the *whyt*. The basic meaning of this term was "tribe," when referring to foreign peoples, and "(clanic) village" in the case of Egypt, a kind of village whose dwellers were linked by family ties. Another term, *menmenet*, "cattle on the move," made its first appearance in the sources of Middle Egypt during this period, so it seems that the new importance of itinerant cattle raising, as well as the movement of mobile populations across the borders of the Nile Valley and the deserts in Middle Egypt, introduced changes in the settlement organization of this region, as *whyt* became then a major feature there (Moreno García 2017). Some scenes in the tombs of this area also reveal that caravans of nomads brought minerals, cattle and other goods from the surrounding deserts. At the same time, localities such as Asyut and Hermopolis historically played an important role as harbors and control points for Nilotic trade, thus strengthening the role of this region as a hub of exchanges. This may explain the frequent mention of Nubians, Asiatics and Libyans in Middle Egypt, sometimes involved in the conflicts that opposed the local authorities to other rulers. Most probably, these populations worked as partners of the local potentates in their trading operations toward the Levant and inner Africa. According to the inscriptions of the early second millennium BC, Bersheh was involved in the trade of myrrh and other aromatic plants, while the decoration of some tombs in Meir and Asyut reproduced Aegean textile patterns. The importance of trade in Middle Egypt, coupled with the interests of its potentates in trading activities, had a deep impact on the regional balance of power and on the conditions of integration of this region in the monarchies that ruled Egypt between 2050 and 1350 BC. Afterward, such a balance of power switched definitively to the profit of Lower Egypt (Moreno García 2017, 2019a).

3.2 Agriculture and Communities in Mesoamerica

In prehispanic Mesoamerica, the temporal coincidence between the transition to sedentary life and the beginnings of plant domestication was less clear than it was in ancient Egypt or Mesopotamia. Maize (*Zea mays*) is the key staple crop in Mesoamerica today, and for most of this cultural region, it was the main food source later in the prehispanic era. The first steps toward maize domestication from the wild teosinte plant occurred before 6000 BC in Central Mexico. Teosinte, which does not have a cob, likely was first exploited for its stalk, which was a source of a sugary liquid, and/or its seeds that, much like maize kernels, can be popped and eaten. Nevertheless, it was not until several millennia after the earliest maize, marked by the recovery of cobs in the archaeological record, that we see the first prehispanic Mesoamerican sedentary communities or villages.

Wild teosinte and early maize seemingly were spread broadly, at an early date, across Mesoamerica's diverse landscape. The addition of maize to cultural niches across the Mesoamerican world, even at a time when populations were largely mobile, may have contributed to the transition to sedentary life that occurred widely and seemingly rapidly across this macroregion between 2000 and 1000 BC. In highland valleys and coastal lowlands, after 2000 BC, ceramics, semipermanent dwellings and other indications of less mobility are evidenced (Clark and Cheetham 2002; Pool 2012). The dating of these archaeological indicators for sedentary ways of life are timed consistently, within less than a millennium, across the entire macroregion (Clark and Cheetham 2002; Rosenswig 2015). Although economically underpinned in part by domesticates in many Mesoamerican regions, the transition to sedentism (and hence the onset of the Formative period) was not purely a subsistence-driven process, since neither the dietary reliance on cultigens nor farming practices by which they were produced were equivalent across regions (Clark and Cheetham 2002; Kennett 2012; Piperno and Smith 2012). Furthermore, if this was merely an outgrowth of local population-resource calculations, why was the timing so consistent across such highly diverse geographic settings? A central tenet then is that this transition, defined by a marked increase in the longevity of settlements and associated landscape investments (Lesure 2008), was a social process to an important extent.

In prehispanic Mesoamerica, the socioeconomic processes associated with the growth in community size and duration were negotiated in different ways through diverse relations and networks. As in ancient Egypt, some communities and settlement networks were dominated by top-down processes, focused on powerful leaders, who personalized their power and operated through transactional networks of kin and allies. Soon after the beginnings of sedentary life, such formations were evidenced in the Gulf Coast, where large stone portrait heads of the powerful stood in central communities (Pool 2012). In other cases, leadership was more faceless, collective and operated with fewer elite trappings both in life or death (Carballo 2016; Pugh *et al.* 2020). Nevertheless, across the Mesoamerican world at this time, central places, larger than surrounding settlements, emerged coincident with or shortly following the advent of sedentary life. These communities interconnected people across regions, and even between regions, through long-distance networks, yet the modes of connectivity were not always the same.

Maize was a key subsistence resource for the people in early sedentary communities across Mesoamerica at this time, albeit to different extents (Piperno and Smith 2012). Beans, squash, avocados, tomatoes and cacao were other key cultigens. In stark contrast to Eurasia and Africa, domesticated animals had a far lesser role. When Mesoamericans first settled in villages, their only domesticated animal was the dog. Turkeys, a second key

Mesoamerican domesticate, only went through this process centuries later. Needless to say, with only those tamed species, beasts of burden did not figure heavily in the prehispanic Mesoamerican world.

The diversity of the climate, landscapes and natural vegetation across Mesoamerica did provide opportunities for a wide array of farming and subsistence practices. Xerophytic plants (such as cacti and other succulents), well adapted to conditions with limited water, were a staple in more arid regions. Economic interdependencies between people who relied on these plants, such as maguey (a source of food, fiber and alcohol) and nopal (a resource for food, which also supported the insect), and communities of maize farmers in certain ways mirrored the Old World relations and economic symbioses between farmers and herders. In lowland regions, Mesoamerican farmers employed mostly extensive horticultural farming techniques that mimicked the environmental diversity of heavily forested regions. But, in certain contexts, more intensive systems of raised fields were constructed. Highland farmers developed an array of water control technologies, intended to supplement rainfall, which often was undependable and temporally and spatially fluctuating. In mountainous and hilly areas, terracing systems were often critical. From early in the history of Mesoamerican farming communities, most agricultural technologies were implemented from the bottom-up and did not necessitate governmental investments or management. Later in the prehispanic sequence, practices, such as the construction of large canals and other means of water control that required more top-down input, were built in certain regions, such as the later Aztec-era water management of the lake system in Central Mexico.

Although early maize, with its small cobs, had low productivity, the plant was highly susceptible to selective pressures, which facilitated adaptation to an array of environmental conditions over time. Selection for larger cob sizes also led to a more productive plant, which had the potential to feed large dense cities and regional populations, which arose in many areas relatively quickly following the formation of villages. Perhaps, in part due to the diverse and, in many ways, unpredictable environmental conditions, exchange and economic interdependence were a key aspect of the prehispanic Mesoamerican economy. When the Spanish arrived in Mexico during the sixteenth century, they were transfixed by the scale of prehispanic markets as well as the diversity of goods exchanged in them (Hirth 2016). They compared them favorably with the markets that they knew in the Mediterranean world, the hub of European commerce at that time. Marketplace exchange and regional market systems were too elaborate to have been new institutions without precedent, and all indications point to their long history in this region and to their centrality for understanding the prehispanic Mesoamerican economy.

Grounded in, but not determined by, environmental diversity and climatic fluctuations (daily, seasonally, annually) and reliant on multiscalar networks and connectivities across multiple scales, the Mesoamerican world was characterized by significant variance in settlement patterns, population and governance across space and time. Most central places and polities were relatively fragile, although notable exceptions did exist, such as Monte Albán, which dominated its region, the Valley of Oaxaca, for more than a millennium. It also is important to point out that, although Mesoamerica often was economically interconnected to different degrees and through distinct modes, it was never politically unified. Late in the prehispanic era, the Aztec politically dominated a significant section of Mesoamerica's Central and Southern Highlands and extended tentacles of domination further afield. Yet, their empire did not encompass even half of the Mesoamerican world, and the nature of their political control was not deep, a factor that contributed to the rapid demise of this imperial domain following the invasion of the Spanish (Berdan *et al.* 1996, Smith and Berdan 2003). Egypt and Mesoamerica thus provide solid ground to explore the emergence and construction of distinctive political structures based on agriculture as well as on trade and specialized craftsmanship.

4 The Beginnings of Complexity: Households, Cities and States

4.1 Centralization versus Local Autonomy in Middle Egypt

The initial impetus in the development of Middle Egypt shares many characteristics with Lower Egypt, especially the Western Delta. This was a relatively vast territory with abundant pasture areas, water and potential agricultural land, crossed by mobile populations and in which kings founded agricultural and administrative centers that constituted islands of authority in a scarcely populated and poorly urbanized territory. Only later, from the final third millennium BC onward, did a distinctive pattern emerge, when several nodes of authority prevailed and were able, apparently, to impose their own conditions on kings in order to accept royal rule and to be integrated into the pharaonic monarchy. Yet, the gradual extension of royal authority in Middle Egypt was hardly a unilateral process that depended solely on the royal will. It was a complex process of negotiation, in which shared interests between pharaohs and local potentates, reinforced by a common high culture, tightened the collaboration between them. Occasionally, however, such interests diverged and inspired separate political paths that usually ended in the division of the kingdom into several rival polities. In such a competitive environment, the potentates of Middle Egypt often promoted their own interests, leading to increasing autonomy. They also forged favorable conditions and alliances that any ruler aspiring to unify and dominate Egypt should weigh carefully if his authority was to be recognized in that section of the Nile Valley (Moreno García 2017, 2018, 2019a).

That Middle Egypt was originally thought of as an idiosyncratic region in Egypt emerges from the analysis of some administrative titles of the second half of the third millennium BC. These titles refer to the "middle provinces," even in one case to the "nine provinces," that apparently encompassed the area between Akhmim in the south to Sharuna in the north. South of this region another toponym, "The Interior of Nekhen (=Hierakonpolis)," designated the eight southernmost provinces of Egypt, those that witnessed the emergence of the monarchy at the end of the fourth millennium BC and that included localities with a high symbolic importance for the crown (Hierakonpolis, Naqada, Coptos, Abydos). From an early date, Middle Egypt played three main roles. On the one hand, it was the seat of powerful families, whose support was crucial for the monarchy, to the point that it was officially recognized in the early documentary and monumental record referring to this region. On the other hand, it represented a sort of "pioneering territory" in which land was abundant and it was possible to expand agriculture and productive activities (quarrying, herding). A third role, much less visible, concerns the strategic position of Middle Egypt as a crossroads of desert, land and fluvial routes, an ideal hub of trade (especially the section of the Nile between Asyut and Bersheh) from which it was also possible to control the circulation of goods between the deserts, the Nile Valley and the Mediterranean (Moreno García 2021).

As stated in the previous section, little is known about the urban layout of Middle Egypt during the third millennium BC, but it seems rather modest and probably secondary with respect to the administrative and agricultural centers founded by the crown (great *hwt*, *hwt*, new agricultural holding). However, these centers administered districts that encompassed several villages, even the house(hold)s of powerful magnates that gave their name to a particular district or territory ("the house of N"). An archive of administrative papyri found at the locality of Gebelein (2500 BC), in southern Egypt, reveals that several villages were part of the allocation ("house of the body") granted by the king to an anonymous official there. Their inhabitants, listed by their names and trades, accomplished diverse services for the administration (mainly building), and it is quite possible that similar conditions also existed in Middle Egypt, as the unpublished papyri from Sharuna list individuals (local potentates?) involved in deliveries of grain for/from the crown. So, the formal integration of Middle Egypt into the administrative organization of the kingdom sought to create centers that controlled districts previously in the hands of local potentates, whereas a regional managerial structure (directed by local officials in charge of the "middle provinces") seems to coordinate this entire region, or at least part of it. Later on, from around 2400 BC, a newly appointed official, the "overseer of Upper Egypt," supervised the collection of taxes and the organization of manpower for the works of the king in Middle and Upper Egypt, but the territorial extent of his authority seems somewhat blurred, sometimes including all of Upper and Middle Egypt and, in other cases, only the eight southernmost provinces of Egypt. Finally, it was from 2350 BC onward that distinguished provincial potentates were granted the title of "great chief of a province." Incorrectly interpreted as a provincial governor, the title served in fact to enhance the position of the dominant potentate (and his family) in a province, a sort of privileged mediator for the crown in local affairs that was thus distinguished from other noble families of lesser rank living in the same area (Moreno García 2021).

The end of the monarchy around 2160 BC witnessed the collapse of this structure of government. For the first time, cities expanded and they and their adjacent areas (called *w* "district") were evoked regularly in the administrative and literary record as the main basis of the territorial organization of the kingdom and the tax system implemented by the crown, especially for the levy of workers. However, their size always remained rather modest when compared with the standards prevalent in Mesopotamia and the Levant (between four and fifteen hectares judging from the very limited archaeological evidence). The sudden importance of cities seems concomitant with the expansion of international trade and, particularly, with fluvial commerce along the Nile, between Nubia and the Eastern Mediterranean and the Near East. Probably not by chance, the new term that appeared at the very end of the third millennium BC to designate a city (*dmj*) means in fact "harbor" or, more precisely, the harbor area of a city (another term, *mryt*, designates both a quay and a market).

This process involved a shift in the balance of power between regions and localities in Egypt, a process still insufficiently analyzed but one that had durable consequences on the organization of the kingdom. It seems quite significant that the growth of organic settlements in Egypt from 2100 BC onward was never followed by the restoration of the former network of productive and administrative centers of the crown (*hwt*) that were so prevalent in the late third millennium BC. Instead, cities replaced the old *hwt* in this role (Moreno García 2019a:22–31, 2019b). Chiefs of cities (or "mayors") now became the main local authorities, who executed the orders or levied the taxes requested by the crown and its agents. Mayors were apparently assisted by an institution badly understood, the "council of a district." As for the old title of great chief of a province, it became very rare and survived principally in Middle Egypt, in provinces such as Qaw, Asyut, Bersheh and Beni Hasan. Given its very restricted geographical scope, it would be excessive to consider their holders as provincial governors. They were probably simply granted a very distinctive honor not shared by other leaders of Egypt, a circumstance that reveals the special status of Middle Egypt and its leaders for the crown in the early second millennium BC. Did cities develop from previous *hwt*? Whereas the names of some localities were formed with the element *hwt*, the excavations did not reveal any trace that the new neighborhoods discovered at localities such as Edfu, Dendera, Elephantine, Abydos or Abu Ghalib grew around a former *hwt*. The expansion of cities then seems to have been an organic process initiated at the very end of the third millennium BC, when no centralized authority ruled over Egypt. Therefore, it was a process that did not obey any royal initiative but was related to the growth of markets and fluvial trade. Markets based on private, noninstitutional trade, production and demand may thus underlay the development of *dmj* and provide a parallel with the importance of markets and trade routes in Mesoamerica (Moreno García 2018, 2019b, 2021).

What is more, the particular status of Middle Egypt seems related to the role played by its leaders in the international trade networks of the Middle Bronze Age. Little is known about the modalities of integration of this region into the newly unified monarchy (about 2050 BC), when the kings of Thebes succeeded in extending their authority all over Egypt. In the decades preceding the reunification, the provincial leaders of Asyut supported the kings of Heracleopolis in their fight against Thebes. The frequent representation of soldiers and besieged forts in scenes from Asyut, Beni Hassan and others, as well as the epigraphic references to warfare, conquest of cities and territories, reveals that warfare was quite common, particularly in the area between Abydos and Qaw that marked the border between Upper and Middle Egypt. So, the apparently soft integration of this region into the Theban kingdom suggests that negotiation was more important that the mere use of force. An important consequence is that the leaders of Bersheh shortly afterward appeared to be in control of the lucrative trade of myrrh and even succeeded to place some of its members in the highest positions at the court. As for the leaders from Beni Hassan, not only did they support the Theban kings against an unidentified enemy in Middle Egypt helped by Asiatics and Nubians around 1990 BC, they also led trade expeditions into Punt and the Levant. It seems then as if the smooth integration of Middle Egypt into the Theban kingdom was rewarded by granting their leaders substantial control over foreign trade. The massive richly decorated tombs that they built, the control of the "gateways" leading to the deserts and to foreign countries (as proclaimed in their inscriptions), and their closeness to the kings point to a considerable degree of autonomy. The frequent depiction of Asiatics, Nubians and Libyans in their tombs (Figure 4), as well as the use of Aegean textile motifs to decorate their burials, suggest that Middle Egypt was a kind of hub of trade that was well connected with Nubia, the Eastern Mediterranean and the surrounding deserts, and that its leaders managed to retain for themselves a nonnegligible part of the wealth of the country. In fact, these elites displayed lavish lifestyles unmatched by other provinces of Egypt (Moreno García 2017, 2019a:168–172, 2019b).

A final consequence of the organic development of cities and their harbor/ market areas and the decline of the old network of *hwt* centers of the crown points perhaps to a somewhat weakened central tax system; the new Theban monarchy that reunified Egypt around 2050 BC was less efficient at collecting taxes. It may also point to an increasing importance of markets and private economic transactions. Quite significantly, more wealth remained in the hands of some provincial elites and of the "middle class" (people who obtained their income independently from the rewards granted by the crown) that flourished then than in previous periods of Egyptian history. Also significantly, individuals began boasting about their possession of ships at the end of the third millennium BC. Trade then appears as a substantial source of wealth for some provincial leaders as well as for the crown, and this explains the massive investment of the crown in the foundation of a network of fortresses/trade centers in Nubia and of the importance of strategic localities that controlled (and taxed?) trade within foreign territories, Elephantine and Avaris/Tell

Figure 4 Asiatic caravan (courtesy of the Egypt Exploration Society)

el-Daba being the most important, but also some localities in Middle Egypt, whose leaders bore titles related to the control of "gateways" into the Nile Valley from abroad (Moreno García 2017, 2019a:168–172, 2021). So, Sarenput I, governor of the caravan and harbor city of Elephantine around 1950 BC, when Egypt was reunified again, claimed that he was *"overseer of all tribute at the entrance of the foreign countries in the form of royal ornaments, to whom the tribute of the Medja-country was brought as contribution of the rulers of the foreign countries,"* as well as *"one who rejoices over the quay/market-place, the overseer of the great vessels of the Royal Domain, who supplies the Double Treasury, the superior of the harbours in the province of Elephantine (so that) what navigates and what moors was under his authority."*

An element of continuity with former periods of Egyptian history is that temples continued to provide legitimacy for the local elites and that, judging from the inscriptions of Hapidjefa of Asyut and other potentates of this region, it was common that they placed their statues there in order to mark their links with the local deities. Kings also found it politically useful to embellish provincial temples, to donate land to them and to place their own statues in local sanctuaries, in all probability as a means to gain the support of the provincial potentates. Their spectacular tombs, not matched anywhere else in Egypt, even rivaling in size and splendor those of kings, are further proof of the very distinctive status of their owners. These Middle Egypt leaders headed considerable retinues and households and were capable of mobilizing hundreds of men when requested by the state (Moreno García 2017). However, shortly after 1800 BC, Egypt entered into a new period of political division about which little is known (see Table 1). It was again a smooth nonviolent process. Kings apparently were unable to have their authority recognized in some areas of Egypt and retreated to the south, into the area of Thebes and the neighboring provinces. Meanwhile the Eastern Delta escaped their authority and became the center of a new kingdom, later to become the core of the Hyksos monarchy. Under these conditions, it is difficult to be precise about the position of Middle Egypt. The great number of kings mentioned in inscribed scarabs and in later lists of kings suggests that the rulers of many localities and/or regions claimed royal status, but this phenomenon seems more intense in Lower Egypt. Around 1600 BC, Meir marked the border between the Hyksos kingdom in the north and the Theban kingdom that ruled the south, just prior to the wars of reunification that culminated with the foundation of a newly unified monarchy around 1550 BC. This suggests that, as it had already occurred five centuries earlier, the elites of Middle Egypt allied themselves with the new royal power that prevailed in Northern Egypt and that was heavily involved in foreign trade, an alliance or collaboration in which Middle Egypt again played the role of the privileged node of trade connecting Nubia and Lower Egypt through the routes of the Western Desert (Moreno García 2019a:168–172, 2021).

4.2 The Complex Articulation of Authority and Political Power in Mesoamerica

In contrast to the Nilotic world, from the onset of village life through the growth of cities during the latter half of the first millennium BC to the eventual rise of the Aztec empire in the last centuries of the prehispanic era, Mesoamerica was not dominated by a solitary core region or a unified dynastic tradition (Blanton *et al*. 1993). Rather, from early on, polities and urban centers continuously rose and fell, regional populations ebbed and flowed, and even the nature of governance was not uniform or consistent over time or space, or even temporally within specific cultural regions (Blanton *et al*. 1996; Fargher *et al*. 2011; Feinman 2018; Feinman and Carballo 2018). Mesoamerica was always a political mosaic, where the fortunes of polities and places were in regular flux (Figure 5). Certain areas, such as Mesoamerica's largest highland valley, the Basin of Mexico, where both the key early city of Teotihuacan and the Aztec capital of Tenochtitlán were situated, were political and demographic cores for much of the history of this macroregion, but not throughout the entire sequence. Other regions, such as the Petén, which was densely settled during the first millennium AD when the temples of Classic-period Maya cities rose above the forested landscape, was much more sparsely populated later in prehispanic times (Sharer and Traxler 2006).

As noted in Section 3, nonresidential buildings and monuments were constructed generally in head towns, which were larger than neighboring communities in many regions, shortly following the establishment of settled villages across Mesoamerica (ca. 2000–1000 BC). At these head towns, a diverse array of spaces and nonresidential structures were defined and built that served to coordinate the community population and often the residents of smaller subsidiary settlements as well (Pool 2012; Pugh *et al*. 2020). In the Maya lowlands, early in the Formative, raised civic-ceremonial spaces may have preceded the construction of permanent residences (Inomata *et al*. 2019). Across the Mesoamerican macroregion, intercommunity and interregional personal and domestic mobility may have continued, even after the advent of sedentary communities in some regions. People likely moved to where there was greater economic opportunity and greater security. From the inception of positions of leadership and structures of socioeconomic inequalities, the constructions of power, its economic

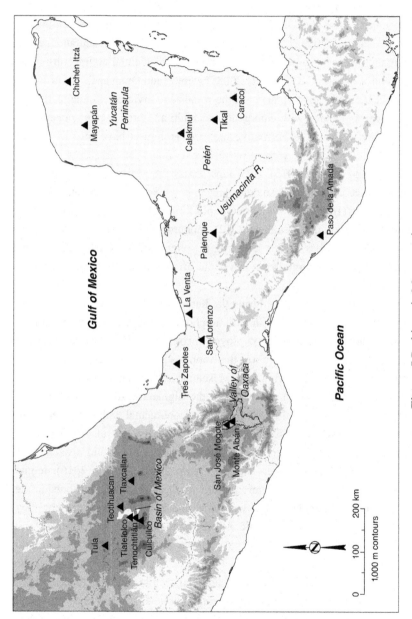

Figure 5 Prehispanic Mesoamerica

underpinnings and how governance was implemented varied markedly over time and space, and these factors prompted episodes of demographic growth and decline during this early period as well as later in prehispanic Mesoamerican history.

As noted, from the beginning of Mesoamerican village life during the Formative period (2000 BC–AD 250), the means and modes of suprahousehold governance were not uniform. For example, nonresidential architecture (e.g., Adler and Wilshusen 1990; Bandy 2008; Peterson and Drennan 2012) provides one critical comparative vantage on the rituals and civic-ceremonial activities that appear associated with emergent leadership and broad-scale cooperation. For the first half of the Formative era, archaeologists have recorded small nondomestic structures with lime-plastered floors at San José Mogote (Flannery and Marcus 2015), E-Groups across the Maya lowlands (Inomata *et al.* 2015), a ballcourt at Paso de la Amada in the Soconusco region of Pacific Coast Chiapas (Hill *et al.* 1998), circular platforms and a carved stone obelisk at Cuicuilco (Plunket and Uruñuela 2012), monumental carved stone heads and tabletop altars/thrones at San Lorenzo (Cyphers and Di Castro 2009), and rectangular plazas and platforms in various arrangements at many settlements (e.g., Carballo 2016).

Civic-ceremonial activities during the Early–Middle Formative period were enacted in distinctive ways, with variation both in how rituals were performed and the scale of the labor efforts deployed to construct nonresidential structures and spaces. One key difference was the emphasis placed on specific individuals in positions of power in parts of the Mesoamerican lowlands (most notably at sites near the Gulf Coast) compared to the highlands. At sites such as San Lorenzo and La Venta, in the Gulf lowlands, monumental sculptures were used to portray charismatic individuals, and these settlements also had palatial residences and elaborate mortuary contexts that are not found elsewhere at that time (Pool 2007; Cyphers and Di Castro 2009; Carballo 2016). Iconic symbols and supernatural imagery were evident more widely, but outside the Gulf, depictions of actual people were rare, and when they were present, they more frequently represent mythic narratives than efforts to legitimize and display personal power (Grove 1999; Grove and Gillespie 2009; Carballo 2016:17). Outside the Gulf centers, Formative ritual precincts tended to be more open and broadly accessible, residential architecture and funerary contexts were less starkly differentiated, and public art portraying individual personages was rare (Grove 2014:182). Given the emphasis on public spaces and buildings, various architectural innovations, including adobes, stone masonry and lime plaster, were evidenced first in these highland regions (Flannery and Marcus 2000:30).

Across Formative Mesoamerica at the outset (or within a few centuries following sedentism in certain regions), there are indications of vertical complexity as evidenced by the emergence of head towns with civic-ceremonial architecture (absent in smaller settlements), distinctions in residential architecture and burials, and differentiation in access to ritual spaces and goods (e.g., Clark and Cheetham 2002; Carballo 2016), but the nature of leadership varied in ways that parallel differences both in other regions after the onset of sedentism (e.g., Renfrew 1974) and at larger scales during subsequent eras in prehispanic Mesoamerica (Feinman and Carballo 2018). At the aforementioned Gulf Coast centers, leadership focused on individuals, who were glorified, legitimized and depicted larger than life in power-laden attire. Elsewhere, for the most part, individualizing rulership was not evidenced at that time and public spaces were prominent.

A key point here is that once head towns and leadership positions emerge, the relevant axis of variation is not between completely bottom-up and top-down governance, but rather it is in the nature of relations between leaders and followers (Ahlquist and Levi 2011). Governance is always relational, and it may take a continuous range of forms, but above scales of several thousands, closely knit networks always have suprahousehold institutions. At one end of that continuum (Blanton and Fargher 2008, 2016; Carballo 2016; Feinman and Carballo 2018) are more collective forms of rule, in which leaders are office holders, subject to checks, balances and limits on their personal clout. Voice and wealth tend to be more equitably distributed. At the other end of the axis are more autocratic, individualizing rulers, who are able to centralize power and wealth, rule through personality cults and face few checks from the rest of the populace. This continuum of ruler–follower dynamics, and its associations with the uses of nonresidential spaces, has been illustrated for Late Postclassic highland Mesoamerican centers (Fargher *et al.* 2011).

Significantly, when the temporal perspective is expanded to the Formative period, it becomes evident that these different modes of governance are not entirely consistent within specific spatial or environmental realms or necessarily across time in a single location. David Carballo (2016) synthesized differences in governance and religious behaviors for the Central Highlands during this era, while Christopher Pool (2007, 2012) noted that not all Gulf Coast regions conformed to the patterns evidenced at San Lorenzo and La Venta. In the lowland Maya region later in the Formative, not all centers adopted modes of individualizing rule at the same time or tempo (Estrada-Belli 2011). Furthermore, at Tres Zapotes (Pool *et al.* 2010) on the Gulf Coast, leadership was initially more in parallel with the individualizing rule at contemporaneous La Venta, but subsequently governance shifted to a more collective formation, in which specific rulers were not depicted ostentatiously and power was shared (Pool and Loughlin 2016). The Formative period Mesoamerican world was a shifting mosaic of many diverse polities that not only varied in their degree of vertical political complexity but also were not uniform in the relational ways they forged coalitions and implemented cooperation. At the same time, these regional political units were linked in macroscalar networks in which innovations, ideas, people and goods were regularly moved (e.g., Rosenswig 2010).

These axes of variation in governance and patterns of aggregation and settlement were evidenced in Mesoamerica's earliest cities as well. Early highland cities tended to be relatively compact and densely settled, whereas early lowland cities were characterized by more dispersed residential patterns. During the Classic period (AD 250–900), Maya cities were governed by kings and their families and retinues, while highland urban centers, such as Teotihuacan and Monte Albán, were characterized by more faceless, less personalized leadership, albeit with seemingly more bureaucratized, institutionalized governmental structures. These axes of variability in Mesoamerican states and cities and comparisons with the Nilotic world are discussed in our next section.

5 Polity and Governance: The Basis of Power and Leadership

A key element in the nature and sustenance of rule and leadership concerns the acquisition of resources – how governance is financed. When access to resources can be monopolized or controlled by those who rule, then rulership tends to be more autocratic with lesser dependence on the trust or compliance of subalterns. Retainers and mercenaries can be coopted by directing the streams of resources that the principals exploit to loyal subjects. Such fiscal streams have been referred to as "external" resources (Blanton and Fargher 2008) as they are not heavily or directly exacted from the local population. Royal estates, control of trade routes, war booty, slave labor and the direct control of spot resources all may be characterized as external resources. Alternatively, when rulers must find ways, such as through taxes or labor drafts, to extract wealth from their local population, then their dependence is on "internal" resources. Such fiscal arrangements require compliance, and so an element of trust, otherwise potential supporters might resist, underproduce or "vote with their feet." As a consequence, governance reliant on internal resources generally coincides with some allocation of voice to a broader segment of the population as well as the provisioning of public goods and services to a wider populace. Dependence on internal resources tends to correlate with checks on power, more even distributions of wealth and lesser degrees of autocracy. In other words, "power over" is reduced, while "power to" is more distributed (Feinman 2002). Tax collection and the bestowal of public goods and services require infrastructure, and so bureaucracy also co-occurs with the reliance on internal resources. In contrast, principals in more autocratic regimes tend to act and relate through interpersonal, transactional networks, principally kin and allies. With such regimes, there are few checks on the power of principals, who endeavor to legitimize their authority through supernatural sanction.

5.1 Middle Egypt: Local Potentates, High Dignitaries and the Royal Court

Middle Egypt, and most particularly the area between Asyut and Beni Hassan, became a center of power closely allied to the monarchy very early on (Moreno García 2013b, 2021). As seen in previous sections, its earliest authorities go back to the beginning of the Egyptian monarchy. These potentates administered the centers of the crown founded there, principally the great *hwt* and the *hwt*; at the same time, this was the only region in Egypt that appears in titles that refer to the property of the kings' sons. One such royal son was buried at Hemmamiya. As for another official, Nykaankh from Tehna, he mentioned proudly in his tomb that pharaohs Menkaura and Userkaf (late twenty-sixth–early twenty-fifth centuries BC) endowed the local temple of goddess Hathor with land (Moreno García 2013b, 2021).

However, there is another base of power, also attested from the earliest times – the "houses" or "domains" of powerful local potentates. So, expressions such as "the house of N," "the domain of N" or, just simply, "N" followed by the hieroglyph sign of a locality sufficed to indicate the territories that supplied goods, taxes and manpower to the royal administration. The interplay between such "houses" and the royal administration was a fluctuating one, and it may reveal the modalities of their formal integration in the kingdom. The inscriptions of Metjen, an official who lived in the first half of the twenty-sixth century BC, show that former "houses" (each one encompassing several villages) were being put under the authority or jurisdiction of great *hwt*, in the context of a reorganization of the territorial administration of the kingdom. So "houses" disappeared as territorial units for almost five centuries, only to become visible again when the monarchy (and its administration) collapsed at the end of the third millennium BC. It was then that toponyms were formed again with the element "house" or that whole regions were named after an anthroponym ("the house of Khuu," Khuu being an official of Edfu).

The mobilization of workers and manpower provides crucial evidence about the weight of these local leaders as well as about their integration into the official networks of power and authority dominated by the king. Thus, when the king ordered Weni to gather a huge army to be subsequently dispatched into the southern Levant (about 2300 BC), it was not "provincial governors" who supplied the contingents but a disparate mix of local authorities: governors of villages, governors of *hwt*, overseers of temples, overseers of grazing areas . . . and "chiefs." When four centuries later, the pyramid of pharaoh Senusret I was built, it was the estates of officials and of simple individuals who provided the workers needed. Other documents, going back from the late third to the middle second millennium BC show that "houses" and individuals delivered workers, taxes and cattle directly to the state. Thus emerges a local world made up of "chiefs," governors of villages, heads of house(holds), potentates and others, who were the real power in the countryside (Moreno García 2013b; Jursa and Moreno García 2015). The most powerful of them were the dominant provincial families that imitated the lavish lifestyle of the court, who provided the royal administration with middle and senior officials, and whose collaboration with the crown was indispensable if kings were to have their authority accepted locally (Willems 2007). Under this social group there existed a world of local subelites integrated by village governors, potentates and wealthy peasants that were part nevertheless of the "great ones" and "great men" mentioned in some texts as opposed to the "modest/humble ones" and "orphans," as if both broad social categories encompassed the majority of the people living in the provinces. Subelites managed the possessions of potentates and temples, headed patronage networks in villages and districts, controlled local life and held modest priestly positions in the provincial temples (Moreno García 2019a:61–108; Grajetzki 2020).

Provincial temples provided legitimacy to local elites and subelites. Their archaeological vestiges in Middle Egypt are surprisingly scarce for the third and early second millennium BC. However, the inscriptions reveal that town deities were crucial in forging personal identities and identification with a community and that kings were conscious of the importance of these sanctuaries, so they struggled to introduce themselves in the dense social networks revolving around provincial temples. The inscriptions from the second half of the third millennium BC reveal that local cults received substantial donations of land from the crown and that kings erected "soul"-chapels in temple enclosures where they put royal statues provided with income (land, offerings, workers: Bussmann 2016; Moreno García 2018, 2021). These works were apparently financed with the taxes collected locally by the crown. Iy-Mery, an overseer of grain and overseer of priests from Akhmim, claimed that he sent grain to the royal residence as part of his tax obligations to the crown and that he used part of it to finance the construction of a royal soul-chapel in his province. Early second millennium archaeological evidence shows that some kings provided decorative items to provincial temples, embellished them and built sanctuaries there. The inscriptions in the tomb of Nykaankh show that control over provincial temples was a truly family affair, a source of wealth, prestige and precious contacts with the crown that served to enhance the social position of the dominant local families, especially as they monopolized the main priestly positions in their respective provinces. Management of the crown's interests (royal agricultural and productive centers like the *hwt*, collecting taxes, organization of the king's works, etc.) was another fundamental source of authority and revenue for these families. The more so as evidence about the origin, composition and weight of the private patrimony of these local elites remains surprisingly scarce. Only at the very beginning of the second millennium BC do some brief statements in the inscriptions of Hapydjefa of Asyut establish a clear distinction between the "house of the father" (the patrimonial possessions of Hapydjefa's family) and the "house of the governor" (the income associated with this administrative position he held: Moreno García 2019a:61–108).

The relations between the two categories of local elites seem based on informal relations of patronage, deference and mutual support (Moreno García 2013b). Governors of villages and "managers" (literally, "overseers of a household") were represented in the tombs of the dominant provincial families as being part of their retinues. Yet the submissive attitude of these subelites, as it transpires from the iconography, may be somewhat misleading. So, a priest like Sobekaa boasting about having served noblemen and overseers of Upper Egypt at the end of the third millennium is nothing extraordinary in itself. But, when other contemporary priests and scribes proudly proclaimed that they worked for simple village governors, chiefs and managers, they seem to provide a more accurate picture of provincial society, one that admits the real importance of the subelites that provided the indispensable link between villagers and the dominant local families. Later on, when towns and cities became the main administrative territorial units of Egypt, the role of these subelites became even more visible, as direct providers of workers and taxes to the crown, with no intervention by any other provincial authority. Thus, for instance, mayors delivered taxes to the crown and sent workers to the expeditions dispatched to the quarries by the crown. A final point is that temples constituted again the indispensable arena that promoted the collaboration between elites and subelites at the local level and that served to enhance the status of both before provincial society (Moreno García 2019a:61–108). The Wilbour papyrus (ca. 1145 BC), a land register of thousands of crown and temple fields and their tenants in Middle Egypt, shows a world of modest priests, officials, military personnel, "ladies" and wealthy cultivators that constituted the intermediate social sector between the most powerful families of the region and the rest of the population (Antoine 2014).

5.2 Powerful Families in Middle Egypt and Their Political Strategies

Having in mind this general background, it is possible to follow the strategies followed by some prominent provincial families in Middle Egypt. Their closeness to the monarchy seems based on a particular arrangement: kings needed the support of local authorities in order to implement their policies, to have their authority recognized locally, to collect taxes and to create a network of centers that guaranteed the storage and delivery of supplies to expeditions and agents of the king. The importance of such centers in Middle Egypt seems closely connected to the role of this region as crossroads and a trade hub as well as a source of highly coveted goods such as semiprecious stones. Thus, the fiscal foundation of Middle Egyptian rule was partly based on external resources, which could be monopolized. The involvement of the local elites in trading activities and in the control of the movement of goods across the Nile and in the nearby deserts probably underlies their prominence in the affairs of the kingdom. But, at the same time, these elites were not mere agents of the crown. They sought actively to integrate themselves into the highest positions of the kingdom, to the point that from 2300 BC, some of them became viziers (a sort of prime minister), while others occupied high positions in the royal administration. They also held ritual positions at the funerary temples of the kings, at Memphis, a source of coveted honors and rewards that helped shape a select circle of influential dignitaries close to the king. Under these circumstances, the accumulation of too much power for too long by some of these families might be regarded by pharaohs as a potential menace that they tried to counteract by several means. This may explain why the position of vizier never remained in the hands of the same provincial family for too long. However, when it is possible to follow in detail the historical trajectories of the most prominent families in Middle Egypt, it is apparent that they dominated entire localities and provinces for centuries and that they built up networks of contacts with other provincial families, including through intermarriage (Kanawati 2017; Moreno García 2019a:61–86).

This predominance made these families formidable political actors in their own right, capable of negotiating the conditions of their integration in the kingdom, particularly during and immediately after periods of political fragmentation in Egypt, when several candidates aspired to the throne. One such period was the very end of the third and the very beginning of the second millennium BC. Localities such as Asyut, Bersheh and Beni Hassan became crucial supporters of one of the two kingdoms (based at Heracleopolis Magna) into which Egypt had split from 2160 BC. The fortune of these localities seems based in the consolidation of a prosperous trade axis connecting Nubia and the Eastern Mediterranean through Middle Egypt and the western branch of the Nile in the Delta. It seems that imports of copper (from Cyprus) and textiles (from the Aegean) and exports of aromatic plants, ivory, gold and exotic hides (from northeastern Africa and the southern Red Sea) fueled the exchanges across this axis, in concurrence with emerging actors based at Thebes. When armed conflict finally erupted, the magnates of Middle Egypt supported the Heracleopolitan kings and fought against Thebes, but their loyalties apparently shifted around 2050 BC. It was then that they chose to side with the Theban kings, making the political reunification of the country possible. But such support was hardly selfless. Officials from Beni Hassan and Bersheh kept control of those lucrative commercial activities and seem to have followed their own diplomatic and trading agendas in the Levant, Nubia and the Red Sea, while supporting the Theban kings when their authority was challenged by some unspecified rivals in Middle Egypt. The magnificence of the tombs of the potentates buried at Beni Hassan, Asyut, Bersheh and Qaw seems connected to their position of controllers of the "gateways" of Egypt (Moreno García 2017; Kanawati 2017, 2019).

This was probably a convenient arrangement for all parties between 2000 and 1800 BC. Theban kings got the support and the know-how of powerful families with good connections with some of the most promising and lucrative areas of the Eastern Mediterranean. They also obtained experienced officials that helped rebuild a unified administrative and tax system now covering all of Egypt. Kings also sanctioned the official appointment of selected members of such families as mayors and great chiefs of the cities and provinces in which they resided. As happened in previous centuries, provincial officials developed a twofold strategy. On the one hand, they preserved their own basis of power as well as their control over the provincial sanctuaries. On the other hand, they sought actively to integrate themselves into the administrative and decision-making structures of the kingdom in order to guarantee that their interests remained safe. Judging from the scarce historical information preserved, pro-vincial officials married among themselves and continued sending their sons to the palace to follow a career at the core decision center of the kingdom (Kanawati 2017, 2019; Moreno García 2019a). The fortunes of the potentates of Middle Egypt were thus closely linked to the monarchy and helped it improve the traditional role of Egypt as trade crossroads between northeastern Africa and the Near East. One can judge the closeness of this relationship by the fact that the mayors who ruled the settlement founded by Pharaoh Senusret III

(1870–1831 BC) to accommodate the staff in charge of his mortuary complex at Abydos came from Bersheh and Qaw, in Middle Egypt (Wegner 2010). As for the old prestige title of great chief of a province, it was exclusively held by potentates from Qau, Asyut, Bersheh and Beni Hassan until it disappeared around 1780 BC.

However, the political foundations of the monarchy rebuilt around 2050 BC remained weak, and it seems that a historical tendency then emerged that was called to have a greater impact in the centuries to follow. The increasing importance of commercial activities with the Levant and the Aegean meant that the Eastern Delta began its rise as the main trading hub of Egypt. During the early eighteenth century BC this region finally seceded smoothly from the king's rule and became an independent political entity on its own. The new era of political fragmentation of the country that followed reproduced the conditions prevalent two centuries before. A trading axis based now on the Eastern Delta, Middle Egypt, the oases of the Western Desert, Nubia and the Levant guaranteed the continuity of commercial activities along the Nilotic axis, and the potentates of Middle Egypt seemed allied to the regional kings now residing at Avaris/Tell el-Daba, in the Eastern Delta, with the frontier between their kingdom and the nascent Theban monarchy situated in the area around Meir. When Thebes finally prevailed and managed to reunify Egypt once more (1550 BC), conditions changed definitively. The Eastern Delta kept and increased its position as the major trade hub of Egypt, a position followed by its gradual transformation into the core of the political power of Egypt, when the Ramesside kings transformed the area of Avaris/Tell el-Daba into one of the capitals of the kingdom, called Pi-Ramesses. It is possible that this historical trend may explain some political events that occurred around 1450 BC. It was then that the potentates of Middle Egypt tried to preserve their traditional role as inescapable partners of the monarchy. Some of them displayed, ephemerally, the old title of great chief of a province, and it is possible that the obscure episode of the creation of a short-lived capital at Tell el-Amarna, in Middle Egypt, points to a last attempt to preserve their political influence at the court. The administrative papyri from the late second millennium BC reveal that kings and temples still controlled many agricultural domains in Middle Egypt. But it also appears that the former "national" prominent role played by the elites from this region had now ended. Temples remained their main basis of income and social influence, as in the case of the high priest of Osiris Wenennefer of Abydos, who lived under the reign of Ramesses II. His family dominated the highest priesthood at Abydos for centuries. He also displayed family and "interpeer" connections with many other members of the high society of his time, including holders of prestigious priestly functions and eminent dignitaries of the court of Ramesses II. As for his wife, she came from a line of high officials rooted at Asyut. Finally, erecting royal statues richly endowed with land and offerings was a privileged means to display the importance of such connections and to strengthen ties with the king himself (Moreno García 2018, 2019a:163–186). Yet, the political influence of Wenennefer seems restricted to the provincial sphere.

In the end, Middle Egypt appears as a distinctive region within Egypt from a sociopolitical point of view, but the elites that dominated this area never appear as a compact social group with a strong identity or acting together to fulfill their common interests. Quite the contrary, these elites hardly operated at all as an organized coherent group (a kind of political regional lobby). Instead, each family, rooted in a particular city or province, followed its own strategies and interests in order to assert and expand its authority both at a local and a national level. In all probability, the family links that connected the dominant families of Middle Egypt was a factor that procured cohesion more than any potential shared political strategy. Under these circumstances, kings found the interstices indispensable to seduce, integrate and shape these dominant families and to prevent the emergence of a feudal class thanks to selective grants of awards, distinctions and positions that promoted rivalries both among and inside the dominant families of this region.

5.3 The Political Arena of Mesoamerica

The earliest cities in prehispanic Mesoamerica arose during the last centuries prior to the advent of the Common Era in the two largest highland valleys in Mexico: the Valley of Oaxaca and the Basin of Mexico (Blanton *et al.* 1993, 1999). Both cities grew extremely rapidly early in their histories, at rates that included significant in-migration. What is important about each of these monumental centers is that neither fits the pattern that predominated in Middle Egypt nor the expectation that the governance of preindustrial urban centers would be dominated by highly autocratic rulers. Teotihuacan ultimately reached a population of approximately 100,000 people during the first 600 years of the first millennium AD and Monte Albán at its height between AD 500 and 850 was occupied by more than 25,000 inhabitants (Figure 6). Yet, throughout the histories of these monumental centers, the footprint of despotic rulership and extreme degrees of economic inequality were not expressed.

Both Teotihuacan and Monte Albán were characterized by monumental architecture, broad public spaces and dense populations. For hilltop Monte Albán, military successes and its defensible location were important elements relevant for its foundation at the center of the broad Valley of Oaxaca. From its emergence, agrarian production in and around the capital appears to have been

Figure 6 Map of Monte Albán

key to the city's fiscal foundation. The elite at Monte Albán lived in elaborate residences, but there is no one building that is uniformly recognized as the ruler's palace. Elaborate residences often included subterranean masonry tombs, some with polychrome painted interiors, but the quantities of portable wealth in these graves were much less ample than for the Classic Maya (ca. AD 250–900). Personalized depictions of Monte Albán elite were rare, especially given the more than one thousand–year period during which the city dominated its surrounding hinterland. It was not until the last centuries of Monte Albán's hegemony that individualized depictions of rulers were carved in stone and represented in other media at the regional capital and other large settlements that were secondary to it. During these last centuries, the governance at Monte Albán and political organization in the Valley of Oaxaca as a whole transitioned toward more autocratic governance, a change that immediately preceded regional breakdown (ca. AD 800–900).

Teotihuacan (Cowgill 2015; Hirth *et al.* 2020), which grew to be far larger and more monumental than Monte Albán, also had a more widespread impact on the history of prehispanic Mesoamerica (Figure 7). Unlike Monte Albán, Teotihuacan was built on flat land and laid out in alignment of a grid plan. After its initial foundation, the city grew rapidly and some of the immigrants lived in neighborhoods that retained distinct ethnic identities for centuries. Many of the residents of Teotihuacan were involved in domestic-scale craft production, in particular the working of obsidian, although the city's economic underpinning was also dependent on farming. With a heavy reliance on internal resources, Teotihuacan's power structure does not seem to have been heavily centralized, but rather power was distributed. As at Monte Albán, there is no clear agreement on the ruler's residence at Teotihuacan, and there are no depictions or lists of named principals from the site. When well-dressed people are illustrated in mural art at Teotihuacan, they are frequently depicted as participants in processions that included multiple unnamed individuals who are often masked and similarly attired. In some representations, these well-dressed and clearly important personages are giving away food and liquid. There is no evidence of bountiful royal graves at Teotihuacan nor legitimizing depictions of individualized royal rulers.

To foster trade (Hirth *et al.* 2020), Teotihuacan in the first centuries of the Common Era sent emissaries to Oaxaca, the Maya region and other parts of Mesoamerica. At the Maya center of Tikal (Carr and Hazzard 1961), representatives from the Central Mexican city may have supported the accession of certain elite familial lines at the expense of others (Figure 8). At a time of increasing exchange across Mesoamerica, an era of dynastic rule and competition was launched in the lowland Maya region that lasted until an episode of more widespread political collapse (ca. AD 800–900). From roughly AD 250 to 900, the rulers of Maya centers jockeyed for political power across the Petén, as their home settlements rose and fell in dynastic cycles (Sharer and Traxler 2006; Estrada-Belli 2011).

In contrast to Teotihuacan and Monte Albán, Classic Maya rulership tended to be autocratic, forged transactionally through marriage and exchange networks in which political and military alliances were forged. Nevertheless, treacheries and reversals in fortune were not uncommon, and fluctuations in settlement populations and the tempos of monument building took place at many Classic Maya sites. Maya lords erected stelae, marking key events in their life cycles. These carved stone pillars, generally accompanied by lengthy texts, depicted the central figures bedecked in flamboyant attire. The context and

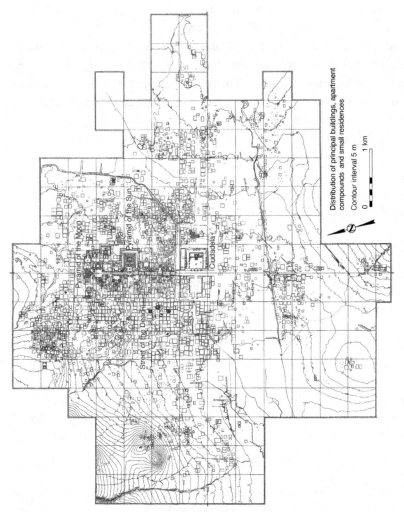

Figure 7 Map of Teotihuacan

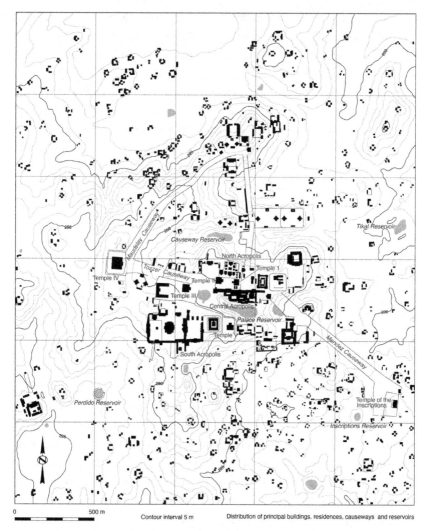

Figure 8 Map of Tikal

central placement of these monuments served to legitimize the rulers whose orders led to their creation. Classic Maya royal palaces were not difficult to identify at most key sites, such as Tikal, Calakmul and Palenque, and their elite tombs were elaborate, often filled with jade, marine shell and other precious goods and adornments. At most Classic Maya settlements, inequities in wealth were expressed (in housing, burials and access to goods) more overtly than at contemporaneous highland cities.

Teotihuacan was depopulated, with ceremonial areas selectively set afire around AD 600 (Cowgill 2015). The Central Mexican city's decline set off an episode of transition that lasted centuries in prehispanic Mesoamerica. By AD 900, not only was Monte Albán mostly abandoned but most of the Maya cities of the Petén were left to ruin. New centers arose across Mesoamerica, and as a consequence, new networks of exchange and interaction across the region were fostered. Ocean-borne trade increased in significance, which contributed to the growth and emergence of new Maya centers in northern Yucatán and along the Atlantic Coast. Rulership in these Postclassic (ca. AD 900–1520) Maya centers was generally less focused on individualized rulers than in the Maya Classic period, as stelae construction ceased.

In Oaxaca (Flannery and Marcus 1983; Feinman and Nicholas 2016), the fragmentation of power evidenced during Monte Albán's last centuries of predominance was followed by the rise of small petty states led by elite families, who ruled relatively autocratically and intermarried with the rulers of other elite lineages across a wide swath of the Southern and Central Highlands. The relative power of individual dynasties and settlements cycled, and no monumental investment in architecture ever again matched the grandeur and scale of Monte Albán in Southern Mexico. Postclassic polities in this region confederated and broke apart as threats and alliances emerged and dissipated.

Further to the north, the site of Tula (Kowalski and Kristan-Graham 2007) arose several centuries after Teotihuacan's fall. Although the settlement never was as monumental or had the macroscale impact of its Central Mexican predecessor, Tula's location at the northern limits of Mesoamerica did provoke greater degrees of interaction with the mobile populations who resided in the desertic regions, which divide Central Mexico from the American Southwest. These increased connectivities (ca. AD 900–1150) spurred southern migrations of desertic peoples, who then moved south through an elongated process, ultimately arriving in the Basin of Mexico, where, centuries later, they integrated into the Aztec empire (ca. AD 1325–1520).

After Tula's fall in the twelfth century AD, Central Mexico was fragmented into many small states, but the proximity of them precipitated competition, conflicts and demands for labor, which likely was one stimulus for regional migrations (Berdan *et al.* 1996; Smith and Berdan 2003). Demographic expansion and political antagonisms fostered agrarian investments across the Basin of Mexico, but especially proximate to the region's lake system. Intensification of market exchange networks underpinned demographic growth and economic connectivity, while providing sources of revenue for the royal rulers of the region's city-states. After centuries during which the fortunes of different local states rose and fell, as larger and larger confederations of these polities rose to power, the Triple Alliance, led by Aztec Tenochtitlán, a city of more than 100,000 inhabitants, eventually came to dominate by AD 1325. From that time until the Spanish invasion (ca. AD 1520), the rulers of Tenochtitlán built the largest empire in the history of prehispanic Mesoamerica, although a significant segment of the macroregion never came under the empire's hegemony.

Over much of its dominion, the Aztec empire left local rulers in place as long as they pledged fealty and paid tribute to the overarching empire. The Aztec political system consisted of hundreds of city-states integrated economically, through intermarriage and other means of interaction. Revenues for the rulers of Tenochtitlán were derived from both external (tribute and taxes leveled on subservient states, rent/taxes to use elite estates) and internal (labor and military drafts, fees for market participation) revenues. At its core in the Basin of Mexico, the Aztec polity established a bureaucratic footprint, but external governance in the provinces tended to be more transactional. Yet, at the same time, a substantial army was marshalled, as military service was mandatory for young men.

The record on Aztec statecraft and political economy is somewhat more robust than for earlier periods in prehispanic Mesoamerica as there is a greater array of empirical sources, including archaeology, indigenous texts and sixteenth–century Spanish accounts. Aztec-era city-states were ruled by kings, but new rulers were chosen by governing councils. Military accomplishments served as one avenue for social mobility, even for those not born into high status. These institutions, councils, the army and the priesthood, as well as the rulers of allied states, could all to a degree balance and check the power of kings, even the ruler of Tenochtitlán.

Overall, prehispanic states in Mesoamerica took a broad range of organizational forms, and there was not continuity in their character within regions. For example, more collectively organized polities in which power was distributed include those centered at Teotihuacan, Monte Albán and in the Northern Yucatán (Chichén Itzá, Mayapán) during the Postclassic period. Alternatively, most Classic Maya polities, as well as the petty states found in Southern Mexico during the Postclassic period were more autocratically organized. Mesoamerica's largest empire, ruled from Tenochtitlán, was somewhat intermediary along this organizational continuum, with elements of both distributed power and rule by kings.

6 State Power and Its Local Implementation

6.1 State Power in Middle Egypt: Taxes and Their Limits

As in any other ancient state, the authority of the pharaohs and their administration left its mark over the territories it controlled, and Middle Egypt was no exception. The most conspicuous thereof was a fiscal geography based on a network of centers of the crown, supported by infrastructural works (harbors, storage facilities, watching points in border areas, roads, etc.) to facilitate a fluid circulation of workers, wealth (including taxes themselves) and agents of the monarchy (Jursa and Moreno García 2015). There were particular building programs (constructing or embellishing temples, erecting statues and chapels), as well as rocks and prominent landmarks inscribed with impressive texts and images that reminded both foreigners and Egyptians of the centrality of the monarchy in the organization of the territory. Yet contrary to common assumptions, the role of the monarchy was very limited in the organization of the irrigation system (in reality left in local hands), so state-promoted hydraulic works remained negligible at best in the consolidation of the monarchy. Finally, kings appointed officials (some of them issued from the very regions that they administered) who introduced in the countryside the codes, values, practices, tastes and lifestyle that prevailed in the royal court and were typical of high culture. In fact, it was not uncommon that kings sent skilled artists to the provinces to decorate the tombs and the monuments of their representatives there. Of course, this was a twofold movement, as local elites adopted these values and used them to display (and strengthen) their closeness to the king and to present themselves as members of the highest decision-making spheres of the kingdom. They also used these values to show their rank and position before the local populations that they ruled, and, occasionally, they introduced subtle innovations in order to assert idiosyncratic values, with a strong local significance but hardly understood elsewhere (Moreno García 2013b). This process was reinforced by their occasional visits to the capital (e.g., as performers of rituals in the funerary temples of the king) and by their interactions with their peers (Moreno García 2006; Bussmann 2016). Of course, the inevitable outcome of such a lavish existence was considerable expenditure, such as costly monuments and precious objects, numerous retinues and local building programs, not to speak of their own residences. All this demanded abundant resources, and access to such resources meant in the end that part of the taxes collected by the royal administration in the provinces were spent in situ, thus contributing to the reinforcement of the status of the local elites as well as their attachment to (and dependence on) the crown (Moreno García 2017).

The earliest structure of the royal tax system in the provinces consisted in the creation of a network of administrative and productive centers (*hwt*, great *hwt*, new agricultural domains, etc.), described in previous sections. It is quite significant that when the network of *hwt* formerly implemented in the third millennium BC disappeared at the very beginning of the second millennium, the sources began mentioning "cities" (*dmj*), quays/markets (*mryt*) and "localities" (*nwt*) instead as the main nodes of territorial organization and tax collecting, probably pointing to a more organic and less centralized articulation of the country. This points to a transition in which much wealth (impossible to quantify) was being produced and circulated outside the economic networks organized and controlled by the crown (Moreno García 2018, 2019b). However, it is also important to notice that the earliest taxing activities of the crown (early third millennium BC) also included "counting" cattle and gold, that is to say, mobile wealth, as if part of the gold extracted and in circulation in the Nile Valley did not depend on the mining expeditions sent by the crown to the deserts. Inscriptions from the middle of the second millennium BC also refer to the deliveries of precious metals (among other goods) that about eighty towns made to Vizier Rekhmire. Temples, in fact, accumulated precious metals that were subsequently taxed by the crown in the late third millennium and in the middle of the second millennium BC. These sacred institutions were thus part of the fiscal geography of the kingdom, as providers of supplies, specialized goods and even workforce, be it "legally" or as the consequence of abuses perpetrated by too zealous (or simply greedy) agents of the crown. The royal annals of the Early and Middle Bronze Age refer to the considerable donations of land that temples received, occasionally accompanied by compulsory workers, even prisoners of war (Jursa and Moreno García 2015). Thus, the decrees of Coptos and the administrative titles present in many inscriptions from Akhmim and Abydos refer to fields and laborers routinely granted to the local temples in order to produce offerings. So, from an economic point of view, temples appear to be sort of managerial agencies, provided with their own fields, herds and workers, capable of storing precious metals (subsequently taxed by the monarchy), enjoying occasional tax exemptions granted by the king and delivering supplies when requested by the king.

As for the nature of the taxes collected, cereals and supplies were perhaps the most important. The inscription of Ibi of Deir el-Gebrawy mentions a field of fifty-five hectares attached to a *hwt*, as well as cattle and personnel, whereas the inscriptions in the quarries of Hatnub mention supplies delivered from some *hwt* to the teams of workers employed there. A papyrus from Sharuna, dating from the twenty-third century BC, records deliveries of grain and dates by a list of men, not necessarily holders of administrative titles. It seems then that crown fields attached to *hwt* produced supplies stored in these centers and that individuals perhaps also contributed with their own deliveries (Moreno García 2013b). For instance, Hapydjefa, a noble from Asyut (early second millennium BC), refers to the first fruits of the harvest that every farmer was expected to deliver to the local temple (Jursa and Moreno García 2015). Another noble from Middle

Egypt, Amenemhat of Beni Hassan, stated that people were expected to deliver grain to him:

> there came years of hunger. Then I plowed all the fields of the Oryx province to its southern and northern border, so that I fed its inhabitants, provided its supplies, and none hungered in it. I gave alike to widow and married woman, and I did not prefer the great to the small in all that I gave. Then came high Niles, rich in barley and emmer, rich in all things, and I did not exact the arrears of the field. (Kanawati and Evans 2016)

However, the main fiscal demand of the crown in the provinces was manpower. Workers were then employed not only in building and quarrying projects but also in military expeditions, and temples also contributed with their own personnel, unless the king granted a specific (and revocable) exemption to a particular sanctuary. Some inscriptions help quantify the burden represented by these demands. An official from the reign of Pepy II mentioned that he went down to the quarries of Hatnub at the head of 1,600 workers, levied from three localities that provided 500, 600 and 500 men, respectively. Later on, Amenemhat of Beni Hassan took part in two mining expeditions far from his province at the head of 400 and 600 conscripts (Kanawati and Evans 2016). These figures stand in comparison with a great quarry expedition sent to Wadi Hammamat that involved the participation of 17,000 conscripts and 20 mayors (an average of 850 men from each locality). The royal decrees of Coptos also reveal that workers were mobilized to perform the "works of the province," to supply the messengers of the king, to accomplish compulsory work in the pastures of the king, to execute transport and digging work, and to deliver gold, copper and precious objects. It is probable that most of this requirement fell on young men, as happens in a famous scene in the tomb of a governor of Bersheh that depicts the transport of a colossal statue. Other institutions (such as "The House of Life") demanded annual requirements of rations and animal feed, offerings, ropes and bindings, and animal skins. Finally, one of the most strenuous tasks consisted of transforming uncultivated and flooded riverside areas into arable fields. According to the decrees of Coptos, flooded areas formerly devoted to pastures were drained and became fields that provided revenue to the temple of the god Min. Khety, a late third millennium BC governor of Asyut, claimed that he had made a sluiceway and a canal that transformed high ground into marshland so that the inundation flooded the mounds and plowlands could be irrigated. He also filled pastures with cattle and built a quay. Later on, around the middle of the second millennium BC, many texts refer to cities as liable to several sorts of taxes, from grain and cloth to precious metals, collected in "quays" that served as tax-collecting points (Moreno García 2019b).

A particularity of Middle Egypt was that cattle raising was a major economic activity there. Officials boasted in their tombs about the enormous herds that they managed and possessed; even cultural particularities, not found for instance in Northern Egypt, were depicted there, like bull fighting. Given the abundance of pasture land and marshes in Middle Egypt, the crown promoted extensive cattle raising there as a means to accrue its revenue, while officials claimed to have expanded cattle production in the areas under their jurisdiction. Thus, Henqu, a governor from Deir el-Gebrawi, stated "I also resettled the towns that were enfeebled in this province with persons of other provinces. Those of them who had been servants, I made their positions into those of official(s) . . . I settled all its mounds with people and cattle [as well as] sheep and goats." Amenemhat, governor of Beni Hassan, gives more details about his duties in this respect:

> I spent the years as ruler of the Oryx nome with all dues for the king's house being in my charge. I gave gang-overseers to the domains of the herdsmen of the Oryx nome and 3000 oxen as their yoke-oxen. I was praised for it in the king's house in every year of the cattle tax. I delivered all their dues to the king's house, and there were no arrears against me in any bureau of his, for the entire Oryx nome labored for me in steady stride. (Kanawati and Evans 2016)

The importance of this activity involved the participation of people specialized in herding, such as Libyans who crossed Middle Egypt with their herds and left their mark in the organization of the landscape. It was at the very end of the third millennium BC that a new kind of settlement called *whyt* "clan, clanic village" was mentioned for the first time, precisely in Middle Egypt, together with the term *mnmnt* "cattle on the move," while Libyans and Nubians were depicted in the elite tombs there, and even "cattle from Retenu [=Palestine]" is mentioned in a tomb. In later times, cattle still remained one of the main sources of wealth of this region (Moreno García 2017). A wooden board from Meir that dates from the middle of the second millennium BC mentions deliveries of cattle to a cargo ship made by several people (Hassan 2016). Cattle matters was also the reason of a conflict between the people of Hermopolis and some soldiers in a letter of the Ramesside period, whereas officials, priests and towns delivered 365 oxen to a temple at Heracleopolis Magna, according to an inscription of the early first century BC (Moreno García 2019a:81–82, 90–91).

What were the limits of the tax system implemented by the crown and of the distribution of wealth between the crown and its local agents? Trade may provide a clue. According to official sources (mostly derived from the crown and its agents), kings controlled the collection of taxes and the distribution of wealth according to a system of remunerations, wages, rewards and occasional privileges that enhanced loyalty, emulation and zeal between the agents of the state. However, things were quite different in reality. Kings built their authority and had their rule accepted in the provincial sphere thanks to the support of the local elites whose loyalty came at a price. This was a changing balance of power based on shared interests and on a complex web of interactions between the provincial and the palatial sphere, including intermarriage between local potentates and the royal family. Control/access to wealth was pivotal to cement the alliance between (and the continuity of) both spheres. Kings asserted their power and their control over local resources by enriching local temples, appointing officials issued from the local nobility and creating centers of the crown (managed by local officials), but they also provided local potentates with considerable income in return for their support. This means that part of the wealth collected by the crown remained in the very areas where it was collected and was used to keep networks (economic, patronage, etc.) whose ultimate beneficiaries were the potentates themselves (Moreno García 2013b, 2018, 2019a:37–60, 2019b). Middle Egypt stands apart from other regions of Egypt during the very late third millennium BC and the first centuries of the second millennium BC for reasons ultimately related to its links with foreign trade. Foreign textiles were proudly displayed in the decoration of some tombs while their owners boasted about their control over myrrh. Officials from Beni Hassan organized missions abroad while, at the same time, they and their colleagues at Bersheh and Qaw managed to control the "gateways" to foreign territories and access to the deserts (and the routes that crossed them). The discovery of inscribed objects of some of these leaders in the Levant, the mutual influence of decorative motifs between the monuments of Middle Egypt and the Levant (as it happened at Tell Burak), and the exceptional representation of foreigners (Asiatic women, Libyan and Asiatic caravans, Nubian warriors) in the tombs of Middle Egypt all point to a close relationship between this region and some areas of the Near East (Moreno García 2017).

In this light, the incorporation of these magnates into the monarchy was probably a careful evaluation of risks and opportunities that also limited the very authority of kings. The end of the Old Kingdom was concomitant with the flowering of Middle Egypt in a context of deeper integration of Egypt into international trade networks. The magnates of Middle Egypt supported the kingdom of Heracleopolis, only to switch sides and accept finally the authority of Thebes, whose kings became the pharaohs of a reunified Egypt around 2050 BC. The price paid by the new pharaohs was considerable: it seems that the magnates of Bersheh now controlled the lucrative trade in myrrh formerly in the hands of Heracleopolis, while the leaders of Beni Hassan continued to be involved in foreign affairs and expeditions to the sources of coveted foreign woods, be it in Punt or the Levant. The enormous tombs built by the magnates of Middle Egypt (Asyut, Beni Hassan, Bersheh, Qaw), not matched anywhere else in Egypt, attest to their extraordinary wealth, while their almost exclusive use of the title of "great chief of a province" and their control of the "gateways" to Egypt and of desert areas suggest that they controlled part of the foreign trade of Egypt. The obvious consequence is that kings retained less wealth than in former periods. They could not or were not interested in restoring the former network of *hwt* centers of the crown, whereas the emergence of a "middle class" (relatively affluent people whose income and economic activities were independent from any service for the state), together with the importance of cities/harbor areas and quays/markets in the inscriptions from this period, confirms that wealth in private hands and circulating through private channels expanded in this period, thus depriving kings of part of the income that in other conditions was destined to them (Moreno García 2013b, 2017, 2019b; Grajetzki 2020). Finally, the elites from Middle Egypt proved to be a crucial support for the monarchy in times of internal difficulties, not matched by potentates from other areas of Egypt. In the end, this was a period in which kings and provincial magnates became instrumental for each other, as expressed in an exceptional statement in the biography of Sarenput I, governor of Elephantine:

> may the gods in charge of Elephantine make endure His Majesty as king for me, may they give birth to His Majesty for me in truth, that he may repeat millions of heb-feasts for me, that they may deliver eternity to him as king and that he may sit on the thrones of (god) Horus, in truth, as I desire.

6.2 Taxes and Politics in Mesoamerica

In stark contrast with Egypt, for most of its prehispanic history, Mesoamerica was not dominated by a unitary, highly centralized polity (Blanton *et al.* 1993). From the emergence of the first head towns and cities, the Mesoamerican world always was a mosaic of polities, with shifting alliances, contestations, and rise and fall in power. Mesoamerican polities illustrate even greater variability in the ways that state power was funded, wielded and manifested than those described for the Nilotic world. Nevertheless, as in Egypt, the specific nature of political power and its implementation was closely linked to the variable economic underpinnings that financed the state and governance at particular places and times. Reliant principally on archaeological, as opposed to documentary, data, the fiscal foundations of Mesoamerican states, with the exception of the Aztec polity, remain difficult to discern. Nevertheless, clues and indicators can be derived from the nature of these prehispanic economies and the diverse ways that Mesoamerican centers appear to have been governed.

As with ancient Egypt, governance in prehispanic Mesoamerica generally did not conform to a long-held conceptual model that was derived from Karl Marx's Asiatic Mode of Production, amplified by Karl Wittfogel's model of hydraulic states and Karl Polanyi's conception of redistributive economies (Blanton and Fargher 2008; Feinman and Garraty 2010; Feinman 2017). In general, governance and rulers in prehispanic Mesoamerica did not directly control economic production or serve nodal roles in centralized systems of distribution. Nor did prehispanic Mesoamerican states depend largely on tribute. For the Aztecs, we know that tribute was exacted from conquered provinces across the empire, but this was only one source of financing for the Aztec state (Smith 2015). Rather, markets, domestic production for exchange, long-distance movements of goods and taxes, including of labor, were all key features of the Aztec and other prehispanic Mesoamerican economies, although their relative importance varied across space and time. The economies and the precise suite of revenues varied from one Mesoamerican state to another, and the ways that power was wielded had much to do with whether economic resources could be tapped and extracted directly by governors or whether it was necessary to derive fiscal support mostly from the local production and the labor of householders.

To consider power, governance and its fiscal foundations in prehispanic Mesoamerica, it is sensible to begin at the end of this era with the Aztecs, as the empirical record, drawn from documentary accounts and archaeology, is the most ample by a considerable degree (Berdan *et al.* 1996; Smith 2015). As noted in Section 5, Aztec governance, even at the height of the empire during the fifteenth and early sixteenth centuries, varied across space. Close to the capital, Tenochtitlán, governance was more bureaucratic with significant investments in infrastructure, while in the conquered provinces, rule was more transactional with local lords left in place, as long as they met their tributary demands and quelled rebellion. Overall, the power of Tenochtitlán's Tlatoani (literally "the one who speaks" or ruler) was somewhat checked by the governors of local city-states that were engulfed by the empire, a parallel, but linked, religious establishment, land-holding kin groups, foreign leaders, who often had dual loyalties, and other institutions. Although the scale of the Aztec empire was far larger than any earlier or contemporary prehispanic Mesoamerican polity, the centralization of power, the degree of autocracy, was intermediate in a continuum of prehispanic Mesoamerican governance along an axis from most-collective to most-autocratic (Feinman and Carballo 2018).

"The Aztecs had a true system of taxation" (Smith 2015:71), which was levied both nearby in the Basin of Mexico and realms closer to the capital as well as in the more distant conquered provinces. These fiscal remittances were taxes, not tribute, as collections were recurrent, regular and based on ongoing commitments. Local taxes took a variety of forms, including on land, labor drafts, including for military service and public works, and collections tied to market participation. These fiscal collections tended to focus on households and individuals. Imperial taxes, levied on conquered lands, were negotiated with subservient rulers and tended to focus on higher-value goods, such as feathers, cloth, minerals and jewels. Demands were placed on subordinate rulers, who bore the responsibility to acquire and bundle the mandated payments.

Given the friction of distance and the differences in tax-collection practices, it is not surprising that the governance of the Aztec polity varied across space. Relatively few public investments were made in distant lands, where local lords were often allowed to remain in power as long as fealty and resource demands were met. Garrisons were established to guard and patrol these lands, sometimes populated by military units drafted from local populations. When unrest occurred or payments were neglected, Aztec armies waged campaigns to resubjugate the local populace.

Closer to Tenochtitlán, governance was more direct, including bureaucratic entities devoted to tax collection and the implementation of public works projects. For example, aqueducts and dikes were constructed in an effort to minimize the flooding of Lake Texcoco at the center of the Basin of Mexico, while causeways across the water were built to facilitate communication. The central precincts of Aztec-period cities, including Tenochtitlán, were carefully planned, maintained and rebuilt. Generally, these core zones followed a grid plan and were characterized by a suite of different administrative and ceremonial structures. At Tenochtitlán, the principal thoroughfares extended out from the city's core zone, dividing the entire settlement into four quadrants. Orientations with cardinal directions were maintained over generations. The planning and architectural implementation of this urban plan must have required significant state investments in material and expertise.

Aztec governance extended to civic-ceremonial institutions, such as temples, including the massive Templo Mayor, which was rebuilt regularly during the roughly two centuries of Aztec imperial rule. Calendric rituals, centered around temples and often accompanied by sacrificial events, also required planning and personnel to enact these ceremonies, which at times were massive in scale. Other ceremonial events were sponsored by Tlatoanis. Military leadership also required specialized positions, which later in the imperial era could either be inherited through noble birth or achieved through military success. Judges, who ensured that the rules of the market were not broached, constituted another bureaucratic realm central to the Aztec state.

The spatial differences in the footprint of governance between the Basin core and outlying provinces parallels certain axes of variability evident in comparisons of earlier Mesoamerican polities. Like urban Tenochtitlán, early highland cities, such as Teotihuacan and Monte Albán, also had monumental central precincts composed of broad gathering spaces and a diversity of forms of prodigious public buildings. Elaborate residences were present at the hearts of these cities as well, but they were not massively greater in size or more centrally positioned than other principal buildings present in the urban cores of these three cities. Temples were the largest structures in these settlements.

Yet in contrast, other prehispanic Mesoamerican cities had a completely different layout, with fewer monumental buildings, smaller plazas and more palace-focused settlement plans (Feinman and Carballo 2018). These centers, such as the Classic Maya cities of the Petén lowlands and the Postclassic Mixtec-Zapotec centers of the Postclassic period, had less bureaucratic but more ruler-centric forms of governance. In general, these latter polities, such as most Classic Maya and Postclassic Oaxaca central settlements were characterized by more dispersed centers, lower expenditures on public goods and less efficient plans of access (lacking wide streets or gridded footprints). The palace of the ruler appears to have been the center for political activity, easily distinguishable from other residences.

These more autocratic polities also tended to be underpinned by economic foundations that were not reliant on broad-based exactions from local farmers and artisan households, but rather on resources that ruling families could more easily monopolize, such as royal landed estates and the control of long-distance trade corridors. We know that the former (estates) were a key bases for the power of the Postclassic Mixtec-Zapotec lords of the Late Postclassic, while dominating access to trade corridors, such as the Usumacinta River, and the luxury goods that were transported down it, was instrumental to the power and wealth of Classic Maya lords. This pattern contrasts with a reliance on internal revenues, derived primarily from the labor and products of local householders, which seems to have been the fiscal grounding for monumental cities, such as Teotihuacan and Monte Albán. These differences in how power was funded and the degrees to which it was distributed or monopolized also affected how rule was legitimated and the ways that power was manifest across landscapes. These matters are considered in the next section.

7 Monumentality and Society

Monumentality conveys a direct sense of the social values and hierarchies, of the nature of political power, of the ideal conception of cosmic and human order, and of the balance between the different actors (including divinities) that constitute any complex society. It also provides clues about where and how social actors invested wealth in order to maximize their social and symbolic capital, a process involving practices as diverse as competition, emulation, euergetism and conspicuous consumption. Finally, as embodiment of the ideological values of these actors, monumentality may also unveil, for instance, the contradictions between absolutist claims for power made by rulers and a more prosaic reality made of "subjects" who enjoyed, in fact, considerable economic autonomy partly invested in wealthy residences. In other cases, intense building programs may be used to assert the symbolic presence of a ruler in areas that escaped largely from their effective authority (Morrison and Lycett 1994; Brunke *et al.* 2016). The presence or absence of substantial public areas (plazas) also points to the importance ascribed to subjects as actors or simply as mere spectators in the ceremonies and expressions of power led by the elites. In this respect, ancient Egypt and Mesoamerica show considerable differences: plazas were an idiosyncratic element in Mesoamerican settlements, as well as pyramid-temples, palaces and neighborhoods formed by residences of considerable size, not necessarily belonging to the elite. By contrast, we know surprisingly little about the palaces and organic residential areas of the elite in ancient Egypt (Tell el-Amarna and Pi-Ramesses are the most important exceptions). Temples were hardly a major architectural feature of the provincial world until well into the second millennium BC (despite the importance of city deities and city sanctuaries in shaping local identities) (Bussmann 2016). As for residential areas, they reveal a marked hierarchy between social groups (as seen at Ilahun) as well as the existence of a sort of "middle class," whereas plazas were conspicuously absent (Moreno García 2019a:35, 148–149).

7.1 Architecture and Ideal Landscapes in Middle Egypt

Funerary architecture stands as the most prominent monumental feature of ancient Egypt (outside the capital) until the middle of the second millennium BC (Baines and Lacovara 2002; Snape 2011:24–104). Grouped in necropolies, the visual impact of tombs and their stratified organization expressed clearly the social hierarchy prevailing in the provincial sphere. It is not surprising then that in times of political turmoil and territorial disintegration, as happened at the end of the third millennium BC, prominent local leaders were "deified" and their monuments (tombs, sanctuaries erected in their honor) became the foci of local cults, loyalties and patronage networks that tied together the local elite and legitimized their authority. The cases of Heqaib (Elephantine), Isi (Edfu), Shemai (Coptos), Idi (Abydos), Medunefer (Balat) and others are conspicuous examples of this cultural trend. In other cases, leaders-to-be thought it useful to express some connection with prestigious rulers of the past, claiming for instance that they had restored the tombs of their alleged ancestors. In any case, the centrality of tombs was such that it took a paramount place in the biographical texts left by many officials of the third and the early second millennium BC. According to these narratives, they boasted about building a tomb (sometimes provided with a basin and trees), about being granted prestigious (and costly) funerary equipment by the king (including architectural items), about paying the artists involved in their construction, even about the concession by the king of a burial area in which the tomb should be erected. Pepiankh "the middle" of Meir claimed for instance:

> I have had the tomb of an official set up right in the necropolis, in the area (called) Nebmaat, in a pure place and a perfect place, where there had been no activity, in which no other ancestor had done (anything). I it was who opened up this area, and it shall function for me as a necropolis and do for me what I desire; I paid great attention to it while I was among the living, and now I have come to it, having grown old most perfectly, having spent my time among the living as a result of being honoured in the sight of the king. (Strudwick 2005:370)

As visual markers of the landscape, provincial tombs attested the power and the closeness to the king of their owners, while the proximity of minor burials to the most important tombs also showed who was who in the local society, the position of individuals in the local hierarchy and their relevance inferred from the decoration and from the location of their tombs in a particular section of a cemetery (Figure 9). It is curious, though, that private residences were rarely depicted in private tombs until the middle of the second millennium BC and that they are hardly mentioned at all in the biographies of their owners. The contrast is blatant with the motifs prevalent in the iconography of private tombs and with the contents of funerary compositions such as the *Coffin Texts*. According to these texts and scenes, their owners represented themselves as rural landlords, ruling over vast domains in which herds, extensive cultivated areas and large numbers of people, involved in many different crafts, were all present under the careful surveillance of the master assisted by his managers, scribes and a diversity of agents (Seidlmayer 2007). The *Coffin Texts* specified that rural manor houses were the center of such domains. Literary texts from the second half of the second millennium BC as well as some residential areas excavated from this period still echo this view, as they evoke an ideal lifestyle made of villas surrounded by gardens and orchards and provided with every kind of agricultural produce. Nonetheless, this was not the case in the literary compositions of the early second millennium BC. In the famous story of Sinuhe, for instance, in which the protagonist recounts his return to Egypt after a long exile in the Levant, it only mentions briefly that the king rewarded Sinuhe with

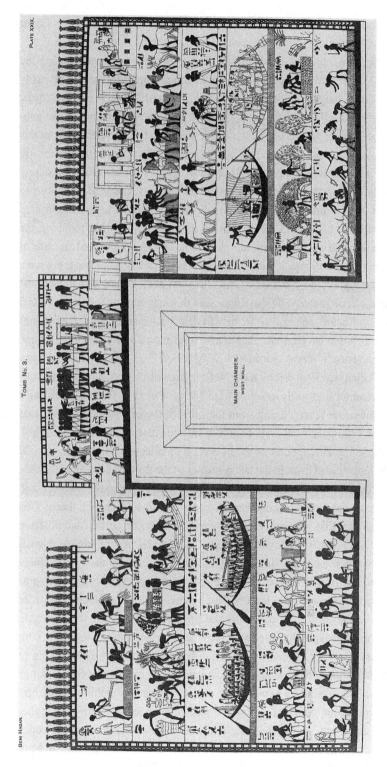

Figure 9 P. E. Newberry, Beni Hassan I, plate 29 (courtesy of the Egypt Exploration Society)

a house and a garden, but it describes in detail the tomb built in his honor together with the luxury equipment supplied by the king to embellish it.

As for temples, their vestiges in Middle Egypt are very scarce during the Early and Middle Bronze Age, to the point that their importance could be easily dismissed and judged irrelevant. However, textual sources provide quite a different picture, because temples figure as prominent elements in the construction of local identities and in the legitimization of the potentates from this region. Royal attempts to mark this region with their constructions are mostly limited to a small step pyramid built close to Zawiyet el-Mayetin and dating from the twenty-sixth century BC (Bussmann 2019), while land donations to royal cults, so prominent in the royal annals of the Old Kingdom, seem limited mostly to Lower Egypt and the area of Memphis. Yet, the inscriptions in the tomb of Nikaankh at Tehna provide invaluable information about the life of a local sanctuary, dedicated to the goddess Hathor. Priestly positions there were virtually monopolized by Nikaankh and his relatives (together with the income in land and offerings derived from them), and this apparently modest provincial cult was significant enough as to benefit from a grant of land (about half a hectare) awarded by King Menkaura and confirmed a few years later by one of his successors, Userkaf (Strudwick 2005:195–199). Another official from nearby Bersheh was honored by King Neferirkare with several courtly appointments, including a priestly position (De Meyer 2011b). Temples were also richly endowed, at least judging from the titles of the overseers of priests that administered the patrimony and wealth of the sanctuaries under their control. According to the inscriptions of the overseers of priests of the temple of god Min at Akhmim, who lived in the last centuries of the third millennium BC, they managed its divine offerings, surveyed its treasury, assigned workers and divided fields into plots, and administered a royal soul-chapel there. This evidence shows that this sanctuary enjoyed an importance that would have otherwise gone easily unnoticed because of the absence of archaeological remains. Meager as this evidence might seem, it in fact shows that local sanctuaries constituted crucial centers that provided both prestige and legitimate authority for provincial leaders. Not by chance, many of them held titles that involved the control of local cults and priests.

Given the huge symbolic valence of provincial temples, they were the setting in which power was negotiated between different actors, each one seeking to enhance his position in the local sphere. According to the royal ideology, kings were the unique mediators between the divine and human realms, assisted by priests. But in areas situated far from the capital, local leaders enjoyed a higher degree of autonomy, while the weight of the cultural and ideological codes dominant at the palatial centers were less pressing. That is why they did not hesitate to claim that divinities favored them directly, without any mediation by the king, and that for these reasons they accomplished rites that put them into direct contact with the divinity. The inscription of Pepiankh "the middle" of Meir is a good example of such claims: "I am a justified one in the sight of the king and in the sight of the god; all things I have are excellent as a result of being a pure-priest of Hathor mistress of Qis (=Meir), and because of doing guard duty for the goddess so that she has favored me" (Strudwick 2005:370). So, even if provincial sanctuaries seem to be very modest constructions in Middle Egypt during the third millennium BC, pharaohs did not hesitate to assert their presence there. Land donations was one such tool that enabled kings to meddle in local affairs and to penetrate the dense networks of power revolving around these cult spaces through very selective grants of fields. The erection of chapels to host statues of the king was another tool. Inscriptions from the third millennium BC show that they were built at Middle Egypt sites such as Akhmim, Asyut, Meir and Zawiyet el-Mayetin.

Things changed little in subsequent periods. King Mentuhotep II, who reunified Egypt around 2050 BC, embellished many provincial sanctuaries in Upper Egypt, but only in areas under firm Theban control, from Abydos in the north to Elephantine in the south. Kings also built temples in the Memphite region and Fayum, while fragments of a biography found at Lisht, going back to the very early second millennium BC, refers to the construction of several (ritual) enclosures at Buto (Delta), Memphis and Oxyrhynchus (160 kilometers south of Cairo), thus leaving a "gap" of royal interventions covering most of Middle Egypt. Only the discovery of a limestone gateway from a temple at Hermopolis, inscribed for Amenemhat II (1911–1877 BC), shows some trace of royal involvement in this region in the first centuries of the second millennium BC (Oppenheim *et al.* 2015).

Under these circumstances, it is notable that this was precisely the very area in which local affairs remained in the hands of very powerful families whose stranglehold over the local sanctuaries remained unchallenged. It was there that practically all of the holders of the title of great chief of a province lived from 2000 BC onward, it was there that traces of royal monuments or of royal involvement in the decoration of local temples is practically absent, and, finally, it is also there that the tombs of the great chiefs represented by far the most outstanding monumental and visual element in the landscape. Their huge dimensions, visually strategic location and lavish decoration conferred them an almost royal allure, while the pride put on their construction and decoration shows unequivocally their symbolic centrality for their owners (Moreno García 2017). Suffice it to mention, for instance, the scene in the tomb of Djehutihotep of Bersheh that represents the transport of a colossal statue not for the king but for Djehutihotep himself. The inscription that accompanies this unique depiction emphasizes that the statue was related to the construction and decorative program of Djehutihotep's tomb (Monnier 2020). As for other owners of some of the richest and biggest tombs known in Middle Egypt, they claimed in their inscriptions their close involvement in temple affairs. That was, for instance, the case of Hapidjefa of Asyut, who inscribed his tomb with a series of contracts, aiming to endow the cult of his funerary statue with offerings in the temples of the gods Anubis and Wepwawet, which he also rebuilt. Ahanakhte of Bersheh boasted in his biographical account about the construction of monuments for the god Thot, the provision of offerings for its cult and his accomplishment of ritual duties (Grajetzki 2012, 151), whereas Khnumhotep II of Beni Hassan expressed in the inscriptions of his tomb the crucial importance of tombs and temples as pivotal in the construction of symbolic landscapes that strengthened (and legitimized) the authority of their builders in Middle Egypt (Kanawati and Evans 2014, 31–36).

7.2 Monumentality in Mesoamerica

As in the world of the Nile, nonresidential structures and at least a degree of monumentality were consistent features of Mesoamerican polities after the advent of sedentary life. But also similar to Egypt, the kinds and scale of the monumentality provides a comparative vantage into the nature of governance, power and how they were legitimized (Blanton and Fargher 2011; Feinman and Carballo 2018). Nowhere in Mesoamerica were tombs, even of the most autocratic kings, as monumental as they were at certain times in Egypt. Likewise, nowhere in prehispanic Mesoamerica did rulers centralize power, especially over broad spatial scales, to the degree reached by the most powerful pharaohs of Egypt. The closest Mesoamerican parallel to the size and wealth of the Egyptian tombs were the subterranean burials (positioned under temples) of Classic Maya kings, who, like the rulers of Egypt, were entombed with large quantities of grave goods and offerings. Classic Maya lords were legitimized like Egyptian kings through lineal descent. They centralized power and ruled autocratically, yet their realms or spheres of hegemony were generally much smaller than for the most powerful rulers in the Nile Valley. So, the size and scope of Classic Maya funerary temples, built to memorialize the reigns and supernatural connections of their rulers, were far less massive than the giant pyramids of Old Kingdom Egypt.

Most prehispanic Mesoamerican leaders, even those less autocratic than Classic Maya rulers, were commemorated at death, and in ways that distinguished them from the bulk of the populace. For example, in the Valley of

Oaxaca during the Classic period, when rule was less autocratic than in the neighboring Maya region, important individuals were buried in subterranean masonry tombs that were placed under the rooms of their elaborate residences. Commoners also tended to be interred in underground cists and tombs at that time, yet the houses as well as the mortuary features were smaller and less elaborately built. Although some Mesoamerican burial contexts were ostentatiously grand, such as lord Pakal's tomb at Classic Maya Palenque, funerary monuments were never the towering feature of Mesoamerican cities and head towns in the manner that such features marked the Egyptian Valley of the Kings.

The monumentality of Mesoamerican centers and cities was marked by temples, palaces, ballcourts, plazas and other civic-ceremonial buildings, although the relative importance and juxtaposition of these structures and spaces was somewhat different in each central place (Feinman 2018; Feinman and Carballo 2018). During the Early and Middle Formative periods (ca. 2000–200 BC), the Gulf Coast (Olmec) was marked by earthen platforms and plaza spaces, but at the largest sites, such as San Lorenzo and La Venta, a distinguishing feature were carved stone heads, which generally are thought to be giant depictions of prominent leaders. Such stone objects are not found elsewhere in prehispanic Mesoamerica, but they do represent a pattern in which those centers dominated by autocratic rulers feature prominent ruler depictions. Later Classic Maya cities featured carved stelae that frequently represented and glorified life crisis events and the victories of the rulers of those communities. Across much of the rest of Mesoamerica during the Early and Middle Formative periods, power was more distributed, rule less centralized, and the earthen and/or adobe platforms that were constructed seem to have been the loci for more communal forms of ritual, although lesser degrees of political and economic inequality were present than evidenced on the Gulf Coast.

Later during the Formative period (after 500 BC), even larger population centers were established across much of Mesoamerica. In the highlands, these early cities tended to be compact, densely settled, with core areas that featured monumental buildings interspersed with open plazas. Compared to earlier centers, cut stone was a more prominent architectural element that was used to face these later platforms and buildings, although the interior cores of the structures generally remained earthen and/or rubble. Some of the most massive structures ever built in prehispanic Mesoamerica were the Pyramids of the Sun and the Moon, which were erected just prior to the Common Era at Teotihuacan (Cowgill 2015). These structures help define the heart of that city and sit along a central avenue, the Street of the Dead, which traverses and, in part, orients the ancient metropolis. Although Teotihuacan was larger than other cities of its time (20 square kilometers and approximately 100,000 people) and more monumental, it was not characterized by either highly elaborate burials or massive depictions or displays of personalized rulers. When important, well-dressed figures were illustrated at Teotihuacan, they often were shown in processions, composed of several similarly dressed and posed figures. In contrast to Classic Maya stelae and the earlier Gulf Coast stone heads, the elaborately attired personages in the Teotihuacan painted scenes were usually masked, and so not individualized. The Pyramids of the Sun and the Moon were giant stone-faced platforms that were thought to serve as foundations for temples.

Temples were the buildings that dominated the Central Mexican landscape during the apogee of Teotihuacan. Civic-ceremonial structures were linked by wide avenues and interspersed by plazas and other open spaces where at least some of the city's large population could periodically gather. There is no clear or uniformly agreed upon ruler's palace at Teotihuacan. Most of Teotihuacan's residences housed multiple domestic units. The pattern was far different at Classic Maya centers, where the ruler's palaces were discernable and distinctive, often situated at the center of the settlement. Plaza or open spaces tended to be less ample, and although there were tall temples, the interior spaces at the tops of these structures were smaller and more exclusive than at Teotihuacan. Classic Maya ballcourts, where the rubber ball game was played, also were relatively small with comparatively little space for spectators. In contrast, at the Late Classic–Early Postclassic Maya center of Chichén Itzá, where there were few stelae that depicted rulers and other indications of more collective forms of governance with distributed power, the main ballcourt is very large and could have accommodated large gatherings.

Variability across prehispanic Mesoamerica in the nature and distribution of monumental structures indicates that while the presence and degree of monumentality yields one set of clues regarding the size of human cooperative arrangements and the presence of suprahousehold means of governance, the specific deployments of monumental structures and space in different historical contexts yield clues about the nature of those socioeconomic formations and how power was distributed in them. In the Olmec and Classic Maya realms, monumentality legitimized and glorified the lives and deaths of key personages, with power concentrated in the lineages associated with those individuals. However, the even greater monumentality of Teotihuacan was not tied to such dynastic figures or specific individuals, rather the built landscape established an architectural setting in which the various neighborhoods, numerous multifamily residential compounds and diverse ethnic populations of the city could move, communicate and join together in ritual efficiently without sharp borders or steep barriers. At Teotihuacan, governance and power appear to have been shared and distributed, tied more to office than lineal descent.

8 Conclusions

In the Lower Nile Valley (Egypt and Nubia) and Mesoamerica, large-scale "worlds" that were linked together by social, cultural and economic ties and affiliations emerged, albeit set in two completely different geographical and ecological settings. These macroscale regions were rarely (or never in the case of prehispanic Mesoamerica) unified politically. Yet, their component polities were organized hierarchically soon after the advent of sedentary life. The polities and populations in both macroregions were interdependent, but in shifting ways, and were key loci for cultural, economic and political innovations. The distinctive trajectories of these past worlds provide an invaluable perspective to view the parallels and differences in the formation and dynamics of complex forms of social, political and economic organizations, which opens very promising arenas for research.

A crucial point is that any determinism, geographical or other, is surely to be rejected. Likewise, neither of these worlds nor their components were marked by simple, unilinear paths of temporal change. Both regions encompassed diverse ecosystems but remained nevertheless culturally and politically idiosyncratic when compared with the areas and peoples situated beyond their borders, usually less populated. Yet, from these conditions, it did not follow that both of them were ineluctably destined to become a political unit or state. As for older historical interpretations that emphasized central control and organization of irrigation and production as primary triggers toward ever-increasing political complexity (with the emergence of kings or lords capable of coordinating work and claiming divine support for their special status), they are no longer valid.

What appears instead is a world of smaller communities, vacillating affiliations and shifting networks (Golitko and Feinman 2015), in which trade and exchanges favored the circulation of goods, people and information, partly under the initiatives taken by political authorities and partly through the agency of a plethora of smaller actors and institutions. Changes in the intensity and directions taken by these circuits left their mark in the fates (rises and falls) of the polities born around them, depending on the ability of rulers to monitor flows of wealth and to shift to new alternative means when available. Absolute power remained thus more an ideal than a reality. In fact, rulers, both in Egypt and in Mesoamerica, were forced to negotiate with local leaders to assert their own authority and to capture substantial wealth, at least to avert the possibility that alternative rival nodes of authority and wealth should arise and challenge or overthrow their power.

Depending on their fiscal basis, kings and rulers deployed their revenues derived from taxes, tributes and other sources as gifts, rewards, symbolic buildings and other practices that established alliances, enhanced their legitimacy, secured fealty and enlarged their retinues. So local communities and small lords kept a substantial capacity to follow their own interests and to limit in a way the interventions of kings and rulers in the local sphere. Thus, interference of central authorities was usually reduced, particularly in areas situated far from the core of the polities that they ruled. As for the volume of taxes and income that they were able to exact, it was irregular. In fact, periods of heavy centralization were often short-lived, and local subelites were successful enough to retain part of the taxes through diverse means, from corruption and royal favor to management of state assets. In all, large-scale "public" works, developed at the initiative of those in power (irrigation networks, roads, expansion of cultivated land, etc.) seem nevertheless rather limited, and they did not justify the alleged redistributive policy inspired by rulers first to set up and later to legitimize their authority.

However, broad-serving investments in infrastructure seem to have been a more significant aspect of Mesoamerican governance than was the case in Egypt. For example, both early urban centers of Teotihuacan and Monte Albán were characterized by urban investments that provided accessways and open spaces for communication and ritual for sizeable segments of the urban populations. Both of these nucleated centers were long-lived and were marked by relatively low degrees of inequity in wealth compared to Egypt and certain other urban centers in Mesoamerica.

In the Nilotic world, any large "constellation of power" was built up by combinations of regional "blocks" gathered together, each one of them, in turn, including smaller "blocks." In the case of the Lower Nilotic area, one can thus discern Lower Egypt, Upper Egypt and Nubia as the main regional blocks, which encompassed subregions with a marked idiosyncrasy, such as the areas of Avaris/Tell el-Dab'a, Memphis, Middle Egypt, Abydos, Thebes, Elephantine and Kerma. In the case of Mesoamerica, the Maya region, the Central Valleys of Oaxaca, the Basin of Mexico and other areas represent distinctive regions, each one also formed by smaller subregions (like the many Classic Maya polities that constituted the Maya world at that time). In Mesoamerica, larger polities emerged from a combination of some (never all) of these "blocks," but imperial political bonds proved to be relatively short-lived experiences. These political affiliations were clearly more durable along the Nile, but not entirely stable across the breadth of time. In contrast, in both of these worlds, a dense network of cultural, religious and economic bonds (fueled often through trade) provided deeper, more resilient linkages that were the basis of cultural identities, symbols and values that forged "Egyptianness," "Nubianness" and "Mesoamericanness" over the long term.

Over millennia, people moved, and polities and governments arose and crumbled, but shared cultural traditions and economic ties tended to be much less fragile.

Yet these broad-brush, general similarities resulted in very different political organizations in Egypt and Mesoamerica. For nearly two thousand years (3100–1069 BC) Egypt remained mostly united in a single state, only punctuated by relatively short periods of political fragmentation (2160–2050 and 1750–1550 BC), an exceptional political achievement when compared with other regions of the ancient world. What was the basis of this astonishing stability? Trade may provide a key and illuminate the different impact it took in Egypt and in Mesoamerica. From a very early date (middle of the fourth millennium BC), Egypt was part of a large network of exchanges that covered northeastern Africa, the Eastern Mediterranean and the Near and Middle East. While relatively reduced in extension and geographically marginal, Egypt was nevertheless a crucial corridor through which African gold and exotic goods, aromatic plants from the southern Red Sea and Egyptian commodities were channelled to the Near East. Several powers struggled to dominate this lucrative territory, until one of them finally prevailed and by 3100 BC Egypt emerged as a unified state. Early pharaohs were thus able to monopolize the access to and the circulation of highly valued goods with relatively little means. No major foreign rival challenged their power, which was highly hierarchical in form, and they never had to face powerful institutions (such as the massive temples of early Mesopotamia) that might have counterbalanced their authority. Nor did they require an extensive bureaucracy to collect taxes or provide public goods. Therefore, early kings enjoyed very favorable conditions to exert their rule and to set up a political structure unusually stable and successful in integrating regional lords and to avoid any major internal challenge.

The monarchy had the ability to build up institutions in which its role was central to implement the material wealth and the symbolic legitimacy that tied the elites closely to the king. Hence, the social and economic reproduction of the elites as *the* ruling group depended in great measure on the favor of the pharaohs, successful enough to avoid any substantial accumulation of private wealth and the emergence of alternative foci of power between 3100 and 2160 BC. In fact, the monarchy set up a network of centers of the crown along the Nile that produced, stored and supplied facilities to the expeditions, officials and workers that circulated around the Nile, as well as to the royal court and the institutions that depended on it (sanctuaries, royal funerary temples). This helped create a "landscape of power" crucial to articulate the territory of the kingdom (cities, on the contrary, were surprisingly small). The monarchy also created logistic bases far from the borders of Egypt proper (at Buhen in

Nubia and the oasis of Dakhla), as well as harbors. As for temples, they were in many cases founded and partly endowed by the monarchy, whereas the tombs and funerary temples of the pharaohs were crucial as providers of prestige, income and social contacts to the provincial and palatial elites. Provincial temples remained modest, but kings granted them land and erected chapels that emphasized their role as patrons. So, the monarchy became the pillar of the economic, political, cultural and territorial organization of Egypt and succeeded in presenting itself as the "natural" and desirable political system, with no *experienced* alternative in view. Whereas some provincial centers gradually grew in importance and wealth, the overall structure of power remained highly oligarchic.

The crown supported some provincial leaders, especially in Middle Egypt, as their interests coincided with those of the monarchy. But this balance of forces collapsed around 2160 BC. Never again was a comparable network of crown centers restored. Instead, cities, harbors and markets/quays along the Nile flourished and replaced them as nodes of territorial organization and taxation. So, the monarchy that reunified Egypt around 2050 BC was very different from its predecessor, a movement that reminds us of the conditions that prevailed in Mesoamerica. Markets and trade were concomitant with a reduction of the power of the kings (even symbolically, as royal pyramids were now smaller and built with poor materials) and with the emergence of a "middle class" whose means of subsistence were independent from the monarchy and who kept substantial wealth (the tax system implemented by the crown was less efficient now). In this new setting, provincial gods and temples became sources of legitimacy and social identity, a role formerly provided by the monarchy. Finally, the deeper integration of Egypt in international trade networks seem to be in part due to the initiative of powerful regional leaders who used the state for their own interests.

The structure of power remained nevertheless deeply oligarchical in nature, and the role of the provincial lords of Middle Egypt seems more important than ever. This may explain why power did not disseminate across society after the period of political division that followed 2160 BC (Moreno García 2019b). Regional lords subsisted and increased their authority instead, whereas the political form restored around 2050 BC was a unified monarchy again. Perhaps the reason was that cities certainly grew then but remained nevertheless very modest in size and population, so they could hardly become counterpoints to either kings or powerful regional potentates. Furthermore, cities hardly modified the dominant social structure of Egypt, based on extended families and patrons. City dwellers were simply part of a social sector that was too small, so their political importance was negligible. Broad-based urban economies dependent on the generative production processes of independent farmers and artisans was never a foundational element of ancient Egyptian polities or economies in the way that such metropoli and their hinterlandss were key to prehispanic Mesoamerica, particularly in the highlands. Nothing like the Mesoamerican plazas was known in Egypt, rather public gatherings tended toward spectacles that legitimized the power of the ruling elite. Evidence about urban bodies in charge of the collective administration of cities is also lacking (cities were ruled in fact by mayors issued from the same dominant families for generations), while pronounced inequalities in house size and access to rations and prestige items confirm that ancient Egypt was generally more unequal than Mesoamerica. Even access to temples was restricted and reserved mostly to the provincial and palatial elites. In the end, vertical bonds prevailed.

In all, power, wealth and social legitimacy (at least as expressed in monumental buildings) took very different paths in Egypt and Mesoamerica from a relatively similar basis in which trade was a crucial element. Yet, for the most part, trade and exchange had a very different character in Mesoamerica. To begin with, given the diverse and topographically jagged landscape of Mesoamerica, the friction of distance there was much greater than in Egypt, where the Nilotic corridor provided a far less rugged path. Furthermore, in the absence of beasts of burden, trade and exchange in Mesoamerica, especially before the expansion of sea trade (ca. AD 800), was largely dependent on human porters, who generally could follow a range of different routes. In general, the monopolization of exchange and trade routes was a much less viable option for Mesoamerican than Egyptian rulers, a challenge magnified by the early significance of marketplace exchange in the former. Significantly, a pattern somewhat more in accord with that in Egypt was evidenced during the Classic period in the Maya region of Mesoamerica, where the exchange of precious, exotic goods along the Usumacinta River could be more readily monopolized (Feinman 2017). There, rulers were self-aggrandizing, invoked an array of strategies to build intraelite alliances, and produced and used valued preciosities to achieve these ends. But the plethora of competing polities along the river and its tributaries provided an impediment to stable, political consolidation. For several centuries, alliances and concentrations of power shifted over time, and central settlements remained relatively dispersed in layout and vacillating in size.

More generally, Mesoamerican production and exchange was more decentralized and not monopolized (top-down) by governmental authorities (Feinman 2017). More typically in prehispanic Mesoamerica, governance and the fiscal underpinnings for it depended on the exaction of taxes and labor from agrarian producers, independent artisans and market participants. Taxpayer compliance was encouraged through the provisioning of public goods and services that fostered commoner residence and participation in close proximity to the centers of power. Thus, prehispanic Mesoamerican cities often were large and nucleated, with layouts that allowed for communal aggregation, ritual and efficient communication. Mesoamerican cities not only had large plazas but also marketplaces, ritual spaces and fortifications that protected large sectors of a community. The Mesoamerican cities characterized by these layouts tended not to have elaborate funerary monuments to royal individuals, public displays that glorified self-aggrandizing monarchs or giant palatial residences (Feinman and Carballo 2018). Rather, Teotihuacan, Monte Albán and even Tenochtitlán all had large central precincts with a diversity of monumental structures of different sizes and forms that appear to have been used by civic-ceremonial bureaucracies that served a diverse array of functions.

From a macroregional vantage, another important difference between the Nilotic and Mesoamerican worlds is that whereas the episode of greatest political centralization in Egypt occurred relatively early in history, this was not the case in Mesoamerica. Rather, the imperial expansion in Aztec times, which still did not encompass the entire macroregion, occurred late in the sequence, the immediate centuries before Spanish conquest. Aztec imperial expansion was financially fueled in part through the governmental coordination with (and partial control of) long-distance traders and exchange as well as taxes exacted from conquered regions. As in Egypt, Tenochtitlán's rulers built and solidified their domain through alliances with and the cooption of local rulers. Mesoamerica's greatest episode of imperial expansion occurred only following the collapse and reorganization of many early cities, polities and regions (ca. AD 600–1000), which seems to have preceded an Aztec-era (ca. 1200–1520) reorganization of macroregional networks of exchange. The relative sustainability or the ultimate potential scale of the Aztec empire is impossible to know, as the hemispheric clash interceded. Yet, the seeming rapidity of Spanish conquest and the help that the invaders from the Eastern Hemisphere received from indigenous subjects of the Aztec domain exposed significant fissures that were already present.

In sum, this multiscalar comparison of these two ancient worlds provides guidance as to how and where to look for relevant parallels in the comparative study of preindustrial times. In contrast to early theorizing on early states and empires, the specific sequences, environments and tempos of change were markedly different and are not fertile grounds for productive generalization. But, at a more middle-ground theoretical tier, there are potentially insightful paths for comparison. In both cases, it is essential to examine change at multiple analytical scales and the processes of hierarchical development and connectivity at the scope of the macroregion may not mirror change at lesser scales. Likewise, and significantly, there also appears to be key parallels between how governance and power were funded and how governance was implemented and power wielded. These parallels have further implications for both the different natures of monumental construction and elite displays as well as the relative degrees of inequality.

Finally, for historical analysis, we conclude by noting several ingrained tenets and presumptions that this comparative effort calls into question. Most notably, we can no longer follow the idea that in preindustrial, particularly non-Western, contexts only ruling elites had agency. Rather, our comparative examination indicates that both secondary elites and subalterns had agency, although the relative impact varies with context. We also question the implicit presumptions that shared cultural affiliations dovetailed with either political polity or biological homogeneity. In lieu of these traditionally presumed yarns, it now seems clear that cultural traditions and behaviors did not neatly covary or shift at a uniform tempo or rate and that genomic variation was not coterminous. The ties of shared cultural affiliations over broad spatial landscapes along with wide-ranging, economic connectivities made regular population movements, both within and between subregions and regions, a consistent element of these preindustrial worlds, which were, if anything, less bounded, with more open political borders than the present. These reconsiderations born from this comparison will hopefully spur reconsideration of key tenets and frames both in the examination of the two macroscale landscapes studied here but also in future and broader comparisons yet to be undertaken.

References

Adler, M. A., and R. H. Wilshusen (1990). "Large-scale integrative facilities in tribal societies: Cross-cultural and Southwestern U.S. examples." *World Archaeology* 22: 133–146.

Ahlquist, J. S., and M. Levi (2011). "Leadership: What it means, what it does, and what we want to know about it." *Annual Review of Political Science* 14: 1–24.

Ando, C., and S. Richardson (eds.) (2017). *Ancient States and Infrastructural Power: Europe, Asia, and America*. Philadelphia: University of Pennsylvania Press.

Antoine, J.-C. (2014). "Social position and the organisation of landholding in Ramesside Egypt." *Studien zur altägyptischen Kultur* 43: 17–46.

Antoine, J.-C. (2017). "Modelling the Nile agricultural floodplain in eleventh and tenth century BC Middle Egypt." In H. Willems and J.-M. Dahms, eds., *The Nile: Natural and Cultural Landscape in Egypt*, pp. 15–51, Blelefeld: Transcript Verlag.

Baines, J., and P. Lacovara (2002). "Burial and the dead in ancient Egyptian society: Respect, formalism, neglect." *Journal of Social Archaeology* 2: 5–36.

Baines, J., and N. Yoffee (1998). "Order, legitimacy, and wealth in ancient Egypt and Mesopotamia." In G. M. Feinman and J. Marcus, eds., *Archaic States*, pp. 199–260, Santa Fe, NM: School of American Research Press.

Bandy, M. (2008). "Global patterns of early village development." In J. P. Bocquet-Appel and O. Bar-Yosef, eds., *The Neolithic Demographic Transition and Its Consequences*, pp. 333–357, Berlin: Springer.

Berdan, F. F., R. E. Blanton, E. H. Boone, M. G. Hodge, M. E. Smith and E. Umberger (1996). *Aztec Imperial Strategies*. Washington, DC: Dumbarton Oaks.

Blanton, R. (1978). *Monte Albán: Settlement Patterns at the Ancient Zapotec Capital*. New York: Academic Press.

Blanton, R., and L. Fargher (2008). *Collective Action in the Formation of Pre-modern States*. New York: Springer.

Blanton, R. E., and L. F. Fargher (2011). "The collective logic of pre-modern cities." *World Archaeology* 43: 505–522.

Blanton, R. E., and L. F. Fargher (2016). *How Humans Cooperate: Confronting the Challenges of Collective Action*. Boulder: University Press of Colorado.

Blanton, R. E., G. M. Feinman, S. A. Kowalewski and L. M. Nicholas (1999). *Ancient Oaxaca*. Cambridge: Cambridge University Press.

Blanton, R. E., G. M. Feinman, S. A. Kowalewski and P. N. Peregrine (1996). "A dual-processual theory for the evolution of Mesoamerican civilization." *Current Anthropology* 37: 1–14.

Blanton, R. E., S. A. Kowalewski, G. M. Feinman and L. M. Finsten (1993). *Ancient Mesoamerica: A Comparison of Change in Three Regions*, second edition. Cambridge: Cambridge University Press.

Brooke, J. L., J. C. Strauss and G. Anderson (eds.) (2018). *State Formations: Global Histories and Cultures of Statehood*. Cambridge: Cambridge University Press.

Brunke, H., E. Bukowiecki, E. Cancik-Kirschbaum *et al.* (2016). "Thinking big. Research in monumental constructions in Antiquity." *eTopoi: Journal for Ancient Studies* 6: 250–305.

Bunbury, J. (2019). *The Nile and Ancient Egypt: Changing Land- and Waterscapes, from the Neolithic to the Roman Era*. Cambridge: Cambridge University Press.

Bussmann, R. (2016). "Great and little traditions in Egyptology." In M. Ullmann, ed., *Ägyptologische Tempeltagung: Ägyptische Tempel zwischen Normierung und Individualität*, Munich, August 29–31, 2014, pp. 37–48, Wiesbaden: Harrassowitz Verlag.

Bussmann, R. (2019). "Zawiyet Sultan in the Old Kingdom – Review and update." In P. Piacentini and A. Delli Castelli, eds., *Old Kingdom Art and Archaeology: Proceedings of the International Conference*, University of Milan, July 3–7, 2017, pp. 196–203, Milan: Pontremoli Editore.

Carballo, D. M. (2016). *Urbanization and Religion in Ancient Central Mexico*. Oxford: Oxford University Press.

Carr, R. E., and J. E. Hazzard (1961). *Tikal Report 11: Map of the Ruins of Tikal, Guatemala*. Philadelphia: University of Pennsylvania, Museum of Archaeology and Anthropology.

Childe, V. Gordon (1950). "The urban revolution." *Town Planning Review* 21: 3–17.

Clark, J. E., and D. Cheetham (2002). "Mesoamerica's tribal foundation." In W. A. Parkinson, ed., *The Archaeology of Tribal Societies*, pp. 278–339, Ann Arbor: International Monographs in Prehistory, Archaeological Series 15.

Cowgill, G. L. (2015). *Ancient Teotihuacan: Early Urbanism in Central Mexico*. Cambridge: Cambridge University Press.

Cyphers, A., and A. Di Castro (2009). "Early Olmec architecture and imagery." In W. L. Fash and L. López Luján, eds., *The Art of Urbanism in*

Mesoamerica: How Mesoamerican Kingdoms Represented Themselves in Architecture, pp. 21–52, Washington, DC: Dumbarton Oaks.

De Meyer, M. (2011a). "Two cemeteries for one provincial capital? Deir el-Bersha and el-Sheikh Said in the fifteenth Upper Egyptian nome during the Old Kingdom." In N. Strudwick and H. Strudwick, eds., *Old Kingdom, New Perspectives: Egyptian Art and Archaeology 2750–2150 BC*, pp. 42–49, Oxford: Oxbow Books.

De Meyer, M. (2011b). "The Fifth Dynasty royal decree of Ia-ib at Dayr al-Barshā." *Revue d'Égyptologie* 62: 57–71.

De Meyer, M., S. Vereecken, B. Vanthuyne, S. Hendrickx, A. Op de Beeck and H. O. Willems (2011). "The early Old Kingdom at Nuwayrāt in the 16th Upper Egyptian nome." In D. Aston, B. Bader, C. Gallorini, P. Nicholson, and S. Buckingham, eds., *Under the Potter's Tree: Studies on Ancient Egypt Presented to Janine Bourriau on the Occasion of her 70th Birthday*, pp. 679–702, Leuven: Peeters.

Estrada-Belli, F. (2011). *The First Maya Civilization: Ritual and Power before the Classic Period*. London: Routledge.

Fargher, L. F., V. Y. Heredia Espinoza and R. E. Blanton (2011). "Alternative pathways to power in Late Postclassic highland Mesoamerica." *Journal of Anthropological Archaeology* 30: 306–326.

Feinman, G. M. (2002). "Five points about power." In M. O'Donovan, ed., *The Dynamics of Power*, pp. 387–393, Carbondale: Southern Illinois University, Center for Archaeological Investigations, Occasional Papers 30.

Feinman, G. M. (2017). "Reframing ancient economies: New models, new questions." In M. Fernández-Götz and D. Krausse, eds., *Eurasia at the Dawn of History: Urbanization and Social Change*, pp. 139–149, New York: Cambridge University Press.

Feinman, G. M. (2018). "The governance and leadership of prehispanic Mesoamerican polities: New perspectives and comparative implications." *Cliodynamics* 9: 1–39.

Feinman, G. M., and D. M. Carballo (2018). "Collaborative and competitive strategies in the variability and resiliency of large-scale societies in Mesoamerica." *Economic Anthropology* 5: 7–19.

Feinman, G. M., and C. P. Garraty (2010). "Preindustrial markets and marketing: Archaeological perspectives." *Annual Review of Anthropology* 39: 167–191.

Feinman, G. M., and L. M. Nicholas (2012). "The late prehispanic economy of the Valley of Oaxaca, Mexico: Weaving threads from data, theory, and subsequent history." *Research in Economic Anthropology* 32: 225–258.

Feinman, G. M., and L. M. Nicholas (2016). "After Monte Albán in the Central Valleys of Oaxaca: A reassessment." In R. K. Faulset, ed., *Beyond Collapse: Archaeological Perspectives on Resilience, Revitalization, and Transformation in Complex Societies*, pp. 43–69, Carbondale: Southern Illinois University, Center for Archaeological Investigations, Occasional Papers 42.

Flannery, K. V., and J. Marcus (eds.) (1983). *The Cloud People: Divergent Evolution of the Zapotec and Mixtec Civilizations*. New York: Academic Press.

Flannery, K. V., and J. Marcus (2000). "Formative Mexican chiefdoms and the myth of the 'mother culture.'" *Journal of Anthropological Archaeology* 19: 1–37.

Flannery, K. V., and J. Marcus (2015). *Excavations at San José Mogote 2: The Household Archaeology*. Ann Arbor: University of Michigan, Museum of Anthropology, Memoir 58.

Gillam, R. (2010). "From Meir to Quseir El-Amarna and back again: The Cusite nome in SAT and on the ground." In A. Woods, A. McFarlane and S. Binder, eds., *Egyptian Culture and Society: Studies in Honour of Naguib Kanawati*, vol. 1, pp. 131–158, Cairo: Conseil Suprême des Antiquités de l'Égypte.

Golitko, M., and G. M. Feinman (2015). "Procurement and distribution of pre-Hispanic Mesoamerican obsidian 900 BC–AD 1520: A social network analysis." *Journal of Archaeological Method and Theory* 22: 206–247.

Graeber, D., and D. Wengrow (2021). *The Dawn of Everything: A New History of Humanity*. New York: Farrar, Straus and Giraux.

Grajetzki, W. (2012). *Court Officials of the Egyptian Middle Kingdom*. London: Bristol Classical Press.

Grajetzki, W. (2020). *The People of the Cobra Province in Egypt: A Local History, 4500 to 1500 BC*. Oxford: Oxbow Books.

Grove, D. C. (1999). "Public monuments and sacred mountains: Observations on three Formative period sacred landscapes." In D. C. Grove and R. A. Joyce, eds., *Social Patterns in Pre-Classic Mesoamerica*, pp. 255–299, Washington, DC: Dumbarton Oaks.

Grove, D. C. (2014). *Discovering the Olmecs: An Unconventional History*. Austin: University of Texas Press.

Grove, D. C., and S. D. Gillespie (2009). "People of the *Cerro*: Landscape, settlement, and art at Middle Formative period Chalcatzingo." In W. L. Fash and L. López Luján, eds., *The Art of Urbanism in Mesoamerica: How Mesoamerican Kingdoms Represented Themselves in Architecture*, pp. 53–76, Washington, DC: Dumbarton Oaks.

Hassan, K. (2016). "An 18th dynasty wooden board in the Egyptian Museum of Cairo JE 95750– CG 25366." *Egyptian Journal of Archaeological and Restoration Studies* 6/2: 125–132.

Hill, W. D., M. Blake and J. E. Clark (1998). "Ball court design dates back 3,400 years." *Nature* 392: 878–879.

Hirth, K. G. (2016). *The Aztec Economic World: Merchants and Markets in Ancient Mesoamerica*. New York: Cambridge University Press.

Hirth, K. G., D. M. Carballo and B. Arroyo (eds.) (2020). *Teotihuacan: The World beyond the City*. Washington, DC: Dumbarton Oaks.

Horn, M. (2017). "Re-appraising the Tasian-Badarian divide in the Qau-Matmar region: A critical review of cultural proxies and a comparative analysis of burial dress." In B. Midant-Reynes, Y. Tristant and E. M. Ryan, eds., *Egypt at Its Origins 5: Proceedings of the Fifth International Conference "Origin of the State, Predynastic and Early Dynastic Egypt,"* Cairo, April, 13–18, 2014, pp. 335–378, Leuven: Peeters.

Inomata, T., J. MacLellan, D. Triadan *et al.* (2015). "Development of sedentary communities in the Maya lowlands: Coexisting mobile groups and public ceremonies at Ceibal, Guatemala." *Proceedings of the National Academy of Sciences* 112: 4268–4273.

Inomata, T., D. Triadan, F. Pinzón and K. Aoyama (2019). "Artificial plateau construction during the Preclassic period at the Maya site of Ceibal, Guatemala. *PLosONE* 14/8: e0221943.

Jursa, M., and J. C. Moreno García (2015). "The ancient Near East and Egypt." In A. Monson and W. Scheidel, eds., *Fiscal Regimes and the Political Economy of Premodern States*, pp. 115–165, Cambridge: Cambridge University Press.

Kanawati, N. (2017). "Ritual marriage alliances and consolidation of power in Middle Egypt during the Middle Kingdom." *Études et travaux* 30: 267–288.

Kanawati, N. (2019). "The royal governors of El-Qusiya in the Old and Middle Kingdoms." In P. Piacentini and A. Delli Castelli, eds.,*Old Kingdom Art and Archaeology: Proceedings of the International Conference*, University of Milan, July 3–7, 2017, pp. 250–259, Milan: Pontremoli Editore.

Kanawati, N., and L. Evans (2014). *Beni Hassan. Volume I: The Tomb of Khnumhotep II*. Oxford: Aris and Phillips.

Kanawati, N., and L. Evans (2016). *Beni Hassan. Volume III: The Tomb of Amenemhat*. Oxford: Aris and Phillips.

Kennett, D. J. (2012). "Archaic-period foragers and farmers in Mesoamerica." In D. L. Nichols and C. A. Pool, eds., *The Oxford Handbook of Mesoamerican Archaeology*, pp. 141–150, Oxford: Oxford University Press.

Kirchhoff, P. (1943). "Mesoamérica, sus límites, geográficos, composicíon étnica y carácteres culturales." *Acta Americana* 1: 92–107.

Kowalewski, S. A. (2019). "Finding marketplaces in prehispanic Mesoamerica: A review." In L. Rahmstorf and E. Stratford, eds., *Weights and Market-places: The Phenomenology of Places of Exchange within a Diachronic and Multi-cultural Perspective*, pp. 323–338, Kiel-Hamburg: Wachholz Verlag & Murmann Publishers.

Kowalski, J. K., and C. Kristan-Graham (eds.) (2007). *Twin Tollans: Chichén Itzá, Tula, and the Epiclassic to Early Postclassic Mesoamerican World.* Washington, DC: Dumbarton Oaks.

Lesure, R. G. (2008). "The Neolithic transition in Mesoamerica? Larger implications of the strategy of relative chronology." In J.-P. Bocquet-Appel and O. Bar-Yosef, eds., *The Neolithic Demographic Transition and Its Consequences*, pp. 107–138, Berlin: Springer.

Millon, R. (1973). *Urbanization at Teotihuacán, Mexico. Volume 1: The Teotihuacán Map.* Austin: University of Texas Press.

Moeller, N. (2005). "An Old Kingdom town at Zawiet Sultan (Zawiet el-Meitin) in Middle Egypt." In A. Cook and F. C. Simpson, eds., *Current Research in Egyptology II*, pp. 29–38, Oxford: BAR Publishing.

Monnier, F. (2020). "La scène de traction du colosse de Djéhoutyhotep. Description, traduction et reconstitution." *Journal of Ancient Egyptian Architecture* 4: 55–72.

Moreno García, J. C. (2006). "La gestion sociale de la mémoire dans l'Égypte du IIIe millénaire: les tombes des particuliers, entre utilisation privée et idéologie publique." In M. Fitzenreiter and M. Herb, eds., *Dekorierte Grabanlagen im Alten Reich – Methodik und Interpretation*, pp. 215–242, London: Golden House Publications.

Moreno García, J. C. (2013a). "Les îles 'nouvelles' et le milieu rural en Égypte pharaonique." *Égypte, Afrique & Orient* 70: 3–12.

Moreno García, J. C. (2013b). "The territorial administration of the kingdom in the 3rd millennium." In J. C. Moreno García, ed., *Ancient Egyptian Administration*, pp. 85–151, Leiden, Boston: Brill, Handbuch der Orientalistik, I.104.

Moreno García, J. C. (2017). "Trade and power in ancient Egypt: Middle Egypt in the late third/early second millennium BC." *Journal of Archaeological Research* 25: 87–132.

Moreno García, J. C. (2018). "Divergent trajectories on the Nile: Polities, wealth and power between 4000–1600 BCE." In H. Meller, R. Risch and D. Gronenborn, eds., *Surplus without State: Political Forms in Prehistory*, pp. 337–372, Halle: Landesmuseum für Vorgeschichte Halle (Saale).

Moreno García, J. C. (2019a). *The State in Ancient Egypt: Power, Challenges and Dynamics*. London, New York: Bloomsbury .

Moreno García, J. C. (2019b). "Marketplaces, customs and hubs of trade in Bronze Age Egypt." In L. Rahmstorf and E. Stratford, eds., *Weights and Market-places: The Phenomenology of Places of Exchange within a Diachronic and Multi-cultural Perspective*, pp. 175–192, Kiel-Hamburg: Wachholz Verlag & Murmann Publishers.

Moreno García, J. C. (2020). "Egyptian agriculture in the Bronze Age: Peasants, landlords and institutions." In T. Howe and D. B. Hollander, eds., *A Companion to Ancient Agriculture*, pp. 173–192, New York, Oxford: Wiley Blackwell, Blackwell Companions to the Ancient World.

Moreno García, J. C. (2021). "Landscape, settlement and populations: Production and regional dynamics in Middle Egypt in the *longue durée*." In T. Schneider, ed., *Gift of the Nile? A Symposium and Workshop on Ancient Egypt and the Environment*, pp. 145–170. Tucson, AZ: The Egyptian Expedition.

Morrison, K., and M. T. Lycett (1994). "Centralized power, centralized authority? Ideological claims and archaeological patterns." *Asian Perspectives* 33/2: 327–350.

Oppenheim, A., D. Arnold, D. Arnold and K. Yamamoto (2015). *Ancient Egypt Transformed: The Middle Kingdom*. New York: Metropolitan Museum of Art.

Peterson, C. E., and R. D. Drennan (2012). "Patterned variation in regional trajectories of community growth." In M. E. Smith, ed., *The Comparative Archaeology of Complex Societies*, pp. 88–137, Cambridge: Cambridge University Press.

Piperno, D. R., and B. D. Smith (2012). "The origins of food production in Mesoamerica." In D. L. Nichols and C. A. Pool, eds., *The Oxford Handbook of Mesoamerican Archaeology*, pp. 151–164, Oxford: Oxford University Press.

Plunket, P., and G. Uruñuela (2012). "Where East meets West: The Formative in Mexico's Central Highlands." *Journal of Archaeological Research* 20: 1–51.

Pool, C. A. (2007). *Olmec Archaeology and Early Mesoamerica*. Cambridge: Cambridge University Press.

Pool, C. A. (2012). "The formation of complex societies in Mesoamerica." In D. L. Nichols and C. A. Pool, eds., *The Oxford Handbook of Mesoamerican Archaeology*, pp. 169–187, Oxford: Oxford University Press.

Pool, C. A., and M. L. Loughlin (2016). "Tres Zapotes: The evolution of a resilient polity in the Olmec heartland of Mexico." In R. K. Faulseit, ed., *Beyond Collapse: Archaeological Perspectives on Resilience, Revitalization, and Transformation in Complex Societies*, pp. 287–309, Carbondale: Southern Illinois University Press.

Pool, C. A., P. Ortiz Ceballos, M. del C. Rodríguez Martínez and M. L. Loughlin (2010). "The early horizon at Tres Zapotes: Implications for Olmec interaction." *Ancient Mesoamerica* 21: 95–105.

Pugh, T. W., E. M. Chan Nieto and G. W. Zygadlo (2020). "Faceless hierarchy at Nixtun-Ch'ich', Peten, Guatemala." *Ancient Mesoamerica* 31: 248–260.

Renfrew, C. (1974). "Beyond subsistence economy: The evolution of social organization in prehistoric Europe." In C. B. Moore, ed., *Reconstructing Complex Societies: An Archaeological Colloquium*, pp. 69–85, Cambridge, MA: American Schools of Oriental Research.

Rosenswig, R. M. (2010). *The Beginnings of Mesoamerican Civilization: Inter-regional Interaction and the Olmec*. Cambridge: Cambridge University Press.

Rosenswig, R. M. (2015). "A mosaic of adaptation: The archaeological record for Mesoamerica's Archaic period." *Journal of Archaeological Research* 23: 115–162.

Scheidel, W. (ed.) (2015). *State Power in Ancient China and Rome*. Oxford: Oxford University Press.

Seidlmayer, S. J. (2007). "People at Beni Hassan: Contributions to a model of ancient Egyptian rural society." In Z. Hawass and J. Richards, eds., *The Archaeology and Art of Ancient Egypt: Essays in Honor of David B. O'Connor*, pp. 351–368, Cairo: Supreme Council of Antiquities.

Sharer, R. J., and L. P. Traxler (2006). *The Ancient Maya*, sixth edition. Stanford, CA: Stanford University Press.

Smith, M. E. (2015). "The Aztec empire." In A. W. Monson and W. Scheidel, eds., *Fiscal Regimes and the Political Economy of Premodern States*, pp. 71–114, Cambridge: Cambridge University Press.

Smith, M. E., and F. F. Berdan (eds.) (2003). *The Postclassic Mesoamerican World*. Salt Lake City: University of Utah Press.

Smith, S. T. (2013). "Revenge of the Kushites: Assimilation and resistance in Egypt's New Kingdom empire and Nubian ascendancy over Egypt." In G. E. Areshian, ed., *Empires and Diversity: On the Crossroads of Archaeology, Anthropology and History*, pp. 84–107, Los Angeles: Cotsen Institute.

Snape, S. (2011). *Ancient Egyptian Tombs: The Culture of Life and Death*. Chichester: Wiley-Blackwell .

Stevenson, A. (2016). "The Egyptian predynastic and state formation." *Journal of Archaeological Research* 24: 421–468.

Strudwick, N. C. (2005). *Texts from the Pyramid Age.* Atlanta: Society of Biblical Literature.

Trampier, J. (2005/2006). "Reconstructing the desert and sown landscape of Abydos." *Journal of the American Research Center in Egypt* 42: 73–80.

Vanthuyne, B. (2016). "Early Old Kingdom rock circle cemeteries in Deir el-Bersha and Deir Abu Hinnis." In M. Adams, B. Midant-Reynes, E. M. Ryan and Y. Tristant, eds., *Egypt at Its Origins 4: Proceedings of the Fourth International Conference "Origin of the State: Predynastic and Early Dynastic Egypt,"* New York, July 26–30, 2011, pp. 427–459, Leuven: Peeters.

Vanthuyne, B. (2018). "The Beni Hasan el-Shuruq region in the Old Kingdom: A preliminary survey report." *Prague Egyptological Studies* 21: 94–105.

Wegner, J. (2010). "External connections of the community of Wah-Sut during the Late Middle Kingdom." In Z. A. Hawass, P. Der Manuelian and R. B. Hussein, eds., *Perspectives on Ancient Egypt: Studies in Honor of Edward Brovarski,* pp. 437–458, Cairo: Supreme Council of Antiquities.

Willems, H. (2007). *Dayr al-Barshā. Volume I: The Rock Tombs of Djehutinakht (No. 17K74/1), Khnumnakht (No. 17K74/2), and Iha (No. 17K74/3). With an Essay on the History and Nature of Nomarchal Rule in the Early Middle Kingdom.* Leuven: Peeters.

Willems, H. O. (2009). "Un domaine royal de l'epoque de Kheops/Khoufou a el-Cheikh Said/Ouadi Zabeida." *Bulletin de la Société Française d'Égyptologie* 175: 13–28.

Willems, H. O., H. Creylman, V. De Laet and G. Verstraeten (2017). "The analysis of historical maps as an avenue to the interpretation of pre-industrial irrigation practices in Egypt." In H. Willems and J.-M. Dahms, eds., *The Nile: Natural and Cultural Landscape in Egypt,* pp. 255–343, Blelefeld: Transcript Verlag.

Yoffee, N. (ed.) (2019). *The Evolution of Fragility: Setting the Terms.* Cambridge: McDonald Institute for Archaeological Research.

To the memory of Marie-Christine Mazé
(January 29, 1954–November 16, 2019)

Cambridge Elements ≡

Ancient Egypt in Context

Gianluca Miniaci
University of Pisa
Gianluca Miniaci is Associate Professor in Egyptology at the University of Pisa, Honorary Researcher at the Institute of Archaeology, UCL – London, and Chercheur associé at the École Pratique des Hautes Études, Paris. He is currently co-director of the archaeological mission at Zawyet Sultan (Menya, Egypt). His main research interest focuses on the social history and the dynamics of material culture in the Middle Bronze Age Egypt and its interconnections between the Levant, Aegean, and Nubia.

Juan Carlos Moreno García
CNRS, Paris
Juan Carlos Moreno García (PhD in Egyptology, 1995) is a CNRS senior researcher at the University of Paris IV-Sorbonne, as well as lecturer on social and economic history of ancient Egypt at the École Normale Supérieure in Paris. He has published extensively on the administration, socio-economic history, and landscape organization of ancient Egypt, usually in a comparative perspective with other civilizations of the ancient world, and has organized several conferences on these topics.

Anna Stevens
University of Cambridge and Monash University
Anna Stevens is a research archaeologist with a particular interest in how material culture and urban space can shed light on the lives of the non-elite in ancient Egypt. She is Senior Research Associate at the McDonald Institute for Archaeological Research and Assistant Director of the Amarna Project (both University of Cambridge).

About the Series
The aim of this Elements series is to offer authoritative but accessible overviews of foundational and emerging topics in the study of ancient Egypt, along with comparative analyses, translated into a language comprehensible to non-specialists. Its authors will take a step back and connect ancient Egypt to the world around, bringing ancient Egypt to the attention of the broader humanities community and leading Egyptology in new directions.

Cambridge Elements ᵇ

Ancient Egypt in Context

Elements in the Series

Printed in the United States
by Baker & Taylor Publisher Services